The INFJ Handbook

A guide to and for the rarest
Myers-Briggs personality type
Second Edition

by Marissa Baker

THE INFJ HANDBOOK: A GUIDE TO AND FOR THE RAREST MYERS-BRIGGS® PERSONALITY TYPE
Second Edition Copyright © 2019 by Marissa Baker
First Edition Copyright © 2015 by Marissa Baker

All rights reserved. This book or any portion thereof may not be reproduced or used in any manner whatsoever without the express written permission of the author except for the use of brief quotations in a book review. For permission requests, write to the author directly through her website:

LikeAnAnchor.com

Cover Design by Marissa Baker. Photo credit: "Cradle of Stars"/Scott Cresswell/Flickr/CC-BY

Second Edition Print ISBN: 9781079928341
Second Edition Digital ASIN: B07WGWZVD4
First Edition Digital ASIN: B010G784QS

Printed by CreateSpace, an Amazon.com Company
www.CreateSpace.com/TITLEID
Also available on Kindle and other devices

Table of Contents

Foreword To The Second Edition	5
Forward To The First Edition	6
Chapter 1: What Is An INFJ anyway?	8
Chapter 2: A Crash-Course In Myers-Briggs®	14
Chapter 3: Worlds In My Head (Introverted Intuition)	22
Chapter 4: Searching For Harmony (Extroverted Feeling)	34
Chapter 5: It's Just Logical (Introverted Thinking)	43
Chapter 6: The Dark Side (Extroverted Sensing)	51
Chapter 7: INFJ Strengths	60
Chapter 8: INFJ Weaknesses	68
Chapter 9: Personal Growth	75
Chapter 10: Things INFJs Want Others To Know	85
Chapter 11: How Other People See INFJs	99
Afterword	107

Foreword To The Second Edition

Much has happened since the publication of my little ebook back in 2015. Traffic to my blog more than doubled, the online INFJ community grew enormously, and the demand for a print edition caught me by surprise. Since it has been several years since the first version and I've grown so much as both an INFJ and a writer, I wanted to bring this book up-to-date before launching it into the world as a physical book.

Those who've read the first edition will find this one offers a much more complete and (I hope) useful description of the INFJ personality type. Every chapter has been updated, re-written, and fact-checked. There are also a few new chapters as well as new stories from INFJ contributors who I hadn't met yet when I published the original book.

Since all my contributors for the first edition were women, I asked INFJ men to contribute to the second edition and several generously responded. I'd like to thank Chase, Jordan, Mark, Michael, Philip, and Roy for sharing their perspectives on being an INFJ personality type with me. Your stories are a wonderful addition to this INFJ Handbook, and I know many readers will benefit from your insight.

Finally, I want to thank all the readers who wrote reviews of *The INFJ Handbook* and who've contacted me to express how much the first edition of this book helped them. Without your support and encouragement this second edition would never have happened.

Foreword To The First Edition

As the rarest personality type on the planet, most INFJs feel like outsiders. We're pressured against our natural inclinations to be more talkative, get out of our own heads, and act like everyone else. Many INFJs grow up thinking "there's something wrong with me," when in reality they are perfectly normal examples of how an INFJ prefers to think and behave. The trouble is, most of us don't know what a typical INFJ looks like and INFJs (as well as the people who know them) often wish INFJs came with a handbook or guide.

For those of you who are INFJs, I hope this book provides reassurance that you are needed and valued just the way you are. For my readers who are not INFJs, I hope this book can serve as a guide for understanding the INFJs in your life. Even though we're rare, about 1 or 2 people in every hundred is an INFJ so you probably know at least one.

I am an INFJ. I've been studying type psychology for about 10 years, and writing about it on my blog for two years. My degree is in English, but psychology is one of my passions. I feel that if we understand how we are similar to other people, as well as how we are different, we'll be able to find common ground for relationships and be more compassionate towards "the other." Just because someone doesn't act or think the same as you is no reason to fear them, or to try to make them conform.

Several INFJs were kind enough to contribute their stories, so this book isn't just going to be me talking. I want to take a moment to say, "Thank you so much. This e-book would have been terribly one-sided without you." To Kerry, who honored me with her honesty in the longest response I received to my request for stories. To Rachel, who I've been acquainted with for years without knowing she was an INFJ. To Johanna, who I've become friends and e-mail "pen-pals" with (I'm so glad you found my blog!). To Denise, who contacted me near the end of my editing process with a story she was so eager to share that it was well-worth it to re-write a few sections. To Yeni, who was brave enough to share her take on INFJ life even though I'm not writing in her primary language. Thanks also to my ENFJ brother, who volunteered to weigh-in on the issue of how other types see INFJs.

That's all for the introductions. Happy reading!

Chapter One

What Is An INFJ Anyway?

I first discovered my Myers-Briggs®[1] type when taking a variety of personality and career placement tests during my last year of high school. At first it was just one more result in a long list. The type description sounded like me, but I didn't realize it went any deeper than other tests like the one that told me I'm a "blue" type.

After entering college with an undecided major and a tendency toward panic attacks, I turned to my library for answers. I found myself in the Dewey Decimal 155.2 (Individual Psychology) section with Susan Cain's *Quiet: The Power of Introverts In A World That Won't Stop Talking* and Elaine Aron's *The Highly Sensitive Person*.

While these books weren't Myers-Briggs® specific, they're what started me on my journey to discover more about my personality. That's when I went back to those four letters, INFJ.

The INFJ Type

There are a total of 16 Myers-Briggs® types. Each type is represented by a combination of four letters: E or I, S or N, F or T, and J or P.

- E/I stands for Extrovert or Introvert. This preference tells us whether we prefer to focus on the outer world (E) or on

---

1 Myers-Briggs Type Indicator, Myers-Briggs, MBTI and MBTI Logo are trademarks or registered trademarks of the MBTI® Trust, Inc., in the United States and other countries.

our own inner world (I)
- S/N stands for Sensing or iNtuition. This describes how we learn information, either by focusing on the real world (S) or by interpreting and adding meaning (N).
- F/T stands for Feeling or Thinking. This is about whether we make decisions by focusing on logic and impersonal criteria (T) or human factors like "How will this make me/others feel?" (F).
- J/P stands for Judging or Perceiving. This process describes whether we prefer structure and planning (J) or openness and flexibility (P) in our outer world.

We'll get into a lot more depth about what these letters mean in the next chapter, but for now that's enough information to start talking about the INFJ type.

The letters I, N, F, and J stand for Introverted, iNtuitive, Feeling, and Judging. This tells us that INFJ types are primarily concerned with the inner world. That's where they are most comfortable and where they gather their energy. Introverted types make up 47-55% of the total population.[2]

INFJs are also Intuitives. They learn new information by looking for patterns, interpreting, and adding meaning. They tend to focus more on the abstract than on taking in information through their five senses. Intuitive types make up about 26-34% of the population.

As Feeling types, INFJs make decisions based on personal criteria. This doesn't mean they're overly emotional. Psychologist Carl Jung, on whose theories the Myers-Briggs® types are based, described both Feeling and Thinking as rational processes because they "hold rational values" and use "differentiated thinking."[3] Feeling types make up 50-60% of the population.

---

[2] Type frequency statistics come from *The Myers & Briggs Foundation*. These numbers represent data about the United States population and are "compiled from a variety of MBTI® results from 1972 through 2002, including data banks at the Center for Applications of Psychological Type; CPP, Inc; and Stanford Research Institute (SRI)."

[3] Evans, Richard. *Jung on Elementary Psychology: A Discussion Between C.J. Jung and Richard I. Evans.* (E.P. Dutton & Co: New York 1976), p. 140.

An INFJ's Judging preference tells us they prefer structure and planning in their outer world. It does not mean they're typically judgmental people or that they're always decisive. Judging types make up 54-60% of the population.

Discovering You're An INFJ

When an INFJ discovers these four little letters it is quite literally life changing. Only about 1-3% of the world's population is INFJ, which makes us the rarest personality type overall.[4] The realization that there are other people out there who are just like you is a great relief. You're not crazy. In fact, you're a perfectly normal INFJ.

> *"When I read the results, I couldn't believe it; it was as if someone had put words to everything I thought was wrong with me. I always felt different from other people, in a bad way. I felt inferior to everyone around me; things came so easily to them, they could verbally express themselves and actually make sense, they were good at sports, they weren't awkward. I was often misunderstood, thanks to my inability to verbalize my thoughts and feelings. I was called 'dramatic' and 'over sensitive' and it was always meant as an insult. So I built a wall to protect myself, and dealt with my intense emotions alone. I had a close friend or two that I could talk to, but that was it. I was very careful about what parts of me I shared with anyone else, fearing that my intensity would scare them off or be totally misunderstood.*
>
> *"I often come across as stupid, oblivious and clumsy. I always believed I was all of those things, until I read my MBTI results. Finally, it all made sense and I immediately started connecting the dots. I am every bit of an INFJ. I have been on a journey of self discovery ever since."*
>
> *–Kerry*

---

[4] When we break it down by gender, INFJ is the rarest personality type for men and the third-rarest for women.

Internet quizzes aren't always accurate but sometimes you'll stumble across one that's close enough to recognize your real type, as Kerry and I did.[5] Once I started looking into my quiz result, everything I read about INFJs sounded so familiar. I learned I wasn't the only person with vivid dreams that seem to blur lines between real and imaginary, or the only person who felt everything deeply and yet couldn't seem to connect with someone in a conversation. My struggles with numbers and difficulty working with concrete facts might be inconvenient, but wasn't abnormal any more. I didn't have to try and ignore my hunches and come up with a logical reason for everything – I could accept the fact that Intuition is how my mind naturally works.

> *"I was having a nice supper with a lady who was the mother of several prominent citizens in town. She was a traveler, moving from state to state as she visited her children and extended family. I was venting a little about a close friend when she suddenly said, "You must be an INFJ," to which I replied, "What's an INFJ?" This lady went on to explain how each of her children had been given the personality test professionally and that talking to me was like talking to one of her sons, who was an INFJ. I went online to find a free test and took it. Sure enough, she was right. Moms are always right. Since then with each new life-change, I have taken the test, and each time it is always the same: INFJ. Reading the descriptions of how INFJs act, think and react to life, I felt a deep sense of relief. I was not the only one. I was not weird. It was okay to be me."*
>
> *–Rachel*

Am I an INFJ?

It's pretty common to mis-type as an INFJ when taking online quizzes. For some reason, certain websites seem skewed toward that result. Further complicating this problem is an abundance of

---

5 If you're looking for a good quiz try personalityhacker.com

online articles talking about INFJs which make them sound like the "best" Myers-Briggs® type, and so people read that and want to label themselves as INFJs. In reality, each Myers-Briggs® type simply describes basic patterns for how different people approach the world. Being an INFJ isn't better or worse than being any other type. It's just meant to describe how certain people's minds work.

So how do you find out if you really are an INFJ? You can take an official test through a certified MBTI® practitioner, who would then have a consultation with you to make sure the test gave you your best-fit result. Alternately, you can take several tests online to compare results and then research the types in-depth to discover which one is the best fit for you.

When we talk about the four functions that make up an INFJ's function stack, we'll get into more detail about how an INFJ thinks and interacts with the world. For now, though, here are a few things that most INFJs have in common and which we typically consider to be key parts of being an INFJ.

Individually, these points are true of more than one personality type. But if most of them sound like you then there's a good chance you're an INFJ.

- Phrases that other people use to describe you include "old soul," "impractical," "daydreamer," "too sensitive," "good listener," "weird," and "deep."
- You have a well-developed "rich inner world" and/or the feeling that you belong in a fantasy world rather than the real one.
- You feel like your mind works in a fundamentally different way than most other people.
- You notice patterns, especially big-picture patterns, that other people typically overlook.
- Conflict is tremendously uncomfortable. If given the option you'll do almost anything to avoid tense moments.
- You feel things deeply but also have an analytical side.
- You can't act on something until it makes sense emotionally and morally, even if it already makes sense logically.
- It seems easy to pick up on other people's emotions and

mirror them while you are talking.
- You can appear to fit-in with most social groups and act as a chameleon in social situations.
- You know a lot more about the people in your life than they know about you.
- Other people want to confide in you, even random strangers.
- You're a spiritual and/or religious person who frequently ponders deep, abstract ideas.
- You are fascinated by personality types and enjoy figuring out what other people's types are.
- There is a struggle between needing to be around people so you can connect with them and share your thoughts, and an introvert's desire for alone time.
- You have a vision for and desire to make the world a better place.
- You feel alienated or not quite human.

Does this sound like you, or perhaps someone you know? Then keep reading. One of the best ways to discover if you really are an INFJ is to see how well you relate to the experiences and descriptions of other INFJs, and that's what you'll find in this book. These descriptions will also help non-INFJs better understand the INFJs in their life.

The INFJ Handbook isn't only written for people hoping to discover their personality type, though. Even if you already know you're an INFJ, my hope is that this book will give you a deeper understanding of your type and offer useful information to support your personal growth.

Chapter Two

A Crash-Course In Myers-Briggs®

When people first discover the MBTI®, they often assume this test simply tells you whether you're an introvert or an extrovert, a Sensor or Intuitive, a Feeler or Thinker, and a Judger or a Perceiver. However, Myers-Briggs® theory goes much deeper than these four dichotomies.

Myers-Briggs® types are based on Carl G. Jung's theory that we're all born with four psychological functions. These functions are a key part of how Myers-Briggs® theory describes complex, nuanced, dynamic personalities. When we talk about "function stacks" in Myers Briggs, we're referring to the mental processes (functions) that people use in a certain preferred order (stack).

Functions are the most complicated aspect of Myers-Briggs® personality types, but they're also what makes it a useful theory for describing how real people's minds work. Most of the time when you see people critiquing Myers-Briggs® they'll stay things like, "People aren't really 100% introverts or extroverts" or "Sometimes I use thinking and sometimes feeling, so the test must be wrong." Function theory is the answer to those criticisms.

I remember feeling very confused when I first learned about function stacks. People start throwing around phrases like "Extroverted Intuition" and "Introverted Thinking" and you wonder what on earth is going on. Then it gets even more confusing when you learn ENxJs don't even use Extroverted Intuition and IxTJ types don't use Introverted Thinking.

In this chapter, I'm going to go through what is (I hope) an easy-to-understand introduction to how functions work. This information is key to understanding what the four letters in a personality type really mean. If you're already familiar with this aspect of Myers-Briggs® theory feel free to skip this chapter.

Intro to Function Theory

There are a total of four basic functions that Jung identified in his research – Sensing, Intuition, Feeling, and Thinking. He described Introversion and Extroversion as "attitudes," one of which we prefer over the other. Each function can be used in an Introverted or Extroverted way, which makes eight functions total that you can have in your personality type.

Isabel Myers and Katherine Briggs built on his theories and developed a method of describing the personalities that result from people using different combinations of functions. They added the Judging and Perceiving attitude to clarify whether a person uses the Judging function (Thinking or Feeling) or their Perceiving function (Sensing or Intuition) to interact with the outer world.

The four letters of a Myers-Briggs® type represent which attitudes and functions someone prefers and how they're used. This results in a 4-function stack for each personality type.[6]

The function that you're most comfortable with is called your primary or dominant function. Personality Hacker calls this the "driver," using the analogy of a car to describe how functions work.[7] Using a different analogy, Lenore Thomson describes our primary function as the captain of a ship.[8] However you choose to describe it, the dominant function is the one that you access most easily and have the greatest proficiency in.

---

[6] To a certain extent, each person uses all eight functions. There are theories describing how our less-preferred "shadow functions" affect our personality, but they don't all agree and I'm not going to get into describing them here. The four functions we'll be talking about are the ones you have conscious access to and are most comfortable using.

[7] Dodge, Antonia. "Personality Development Tools: The Car Model." PersonalityHacker.com. N.p., 13 Aug. 2014. Web. 9 Jan. 2019.

[8] Thomson, Lenore. *Personality Type, An Owner's Manual: A Practical Guide To Understanding Yourself and Others Through Typology.* (Shambhala Publications: Boston 1998), p. 87.

Your secondary or auxiliary function is called the co-pilot in Personality Hacker's car model. This is the term I prefer, so we'll be using co-pilot to refer to the secondary function throughout this book. Thomson describes it as a petty officer who provides an important perspective on how to run the ship.

The tertiary function isn't as well developed as the two higher on your function stack. Personality Hacker describes it as a 10-year-old in the back seat of a car. Thomson calls it a water skier being towed behind your ship shouting remarks that are alternately distracting and useful.

The inferior function is much harder for us to use. It's often outside our conscious control and shows up when we're stressed. Personality Hacker calls this a 3-year-old in the backseat of the car. Thomson compares it to a mutinous crew member that keeps trying to take over the ship.

What J and P Really Mean

Now that we've established a vocabulary for talking about the psychological functions, we can look at how they work in Myers-Briggs® theory. Let's start by talking about what the letters J and P really mean.

Contrary to popular opinion, Judging and Perceiving aren't a sliding scale. They aren't even meant to stand on their own as an aspect of your personality. They're just in your four-letter type to describe how you use your functions.

As I mentioned in the last section, the four functions fit into two groups: Perceiving and Judging. According to Isabel Myers, the perceiving function includes "the process of becoming aware of things, people, occurrences, and ideas."[9] Intuition (N) and Sensing (S) are two different ways of perceiving. They're how we learn and process new information.

The judging function "includes the process of coming to conclusions about what has been perceived."[10] Thinking (T) and

---

9 Myers, Isabel Briggs. *Gifts Differing*. (Palo Alto: Davis-Black Publishing 1995), p. 1
10 Myers, *Gifts Differing*, p. 1

Feeling (F) are two different ways of judging. We use these functions when making decisions.

When you have a J in your Myers-Briggs® type, that simply means you use your preferred Thinking or Feeling process to interact with the outer world. If you're a P type, then you use your preferred Sensing or Intuition process in the outer world.

This is why we describe an NP type as someone who uses Extroverted Intuition and an FJ type as someone who uses Extroverted Feeling. Similarly, TJ types use Extroverted Thinking and SP types use Extroverted Sensing. Whether you're an extrovert or an introvert, the J/P preference always describes the Extroverted side of your personality.

Your First Two Functions

We don't just have an extroverted side to our personalities, though. We're all a mix of both Introvert and Extrovert, though we each have one attitude that we prefer.[11]

If you extrovert your perceiving side (S/N) then your judging side (T/F) is introverted. The opposite is also true. If you extrovert your judging side (T/F) then your perceiving side (S/N) is introverted.

As an FJ type, INFJs extrovert their preferred judging function, (Feeling). That means their preferred perceiving function (Intuition) is introverted. In other words, INFJs use Introverted Intuition and Extroverted Feeling as the first two functions in their stack.

Now that we've found our first two functions, we can start talking about the order we prefer to use them in. For that, it's time to talk about what I and E mean in Myers-Briggs®.

Introverts and Extroverts Explained

The I/E preference in Myers-Briggs® tells you which attitude a person's dominant function has. Every healthy person uses both

---
11 There's no such thing as an "ambivert" in Myers-Briggs® theory. The people who call themselves amiverts are simply more balanced in how they use the Introverted and Extroverted sides of their personalities.

Introversion and Extroversion, but we all have a tendency toward one or the other.[12]

For people with an E in their Myers-Briggs® type, their Extroverted function is dominant. An ENFP, for example, leads with Extroverted Intuition. Their co-pilot function is introverted, in this case Introverted Feeling.

For Introverts, the dominant function is introverted and their co-pilot is extroverted. An ISTP, for example, uses Introverted Thinking as their dominant function. Their co-pilot is extroverted, in this case Extroverted Sensing.

In an extroverted type, their J/P preference matches their dominant function. Introverts, however, use the J/P preference as their co-pilot to interact with the outer world. It isn't their favorite mental process. This means that even though INFJs have a J in their four-letter type, they're actually a dominant perceiving type. We lead with Introverted Intuition (a perceiving function), and Extroverted Feeling (a judging function) is our co-pilot.

The fact that our J/P preference is outer-word oriented is one reason so many online tests don't give accurate results. They're lining-up descriptions of Extrovert-Introvert, Sensing-Intuition, Thinking-Feeling, and Judging-Perceiving and then making you choose where you fall on the dichotomies. That might work okay for extroverts (whose J/P preference matches their dominant function) but these tests often get mixed-up on the J/P preference for introverts (since it does not match their dominant function).

> *"I was typed as either INFJ or INFP. While INFJ was still a more common result for me (I took about 50 tests to make sure), I still had my doubts. This is what made me delve into studying MBTI and cognitive functions on the sidelines, and the more I learned, the more I understood about myself."*
>
> *– Denise*

---

[12] Jung himself said, "There is no such thing as a pure extrovert or a pure introvert. Such a man would be in the lunatic asylum." Evans, *Jung on Elementary Psychology*, p. 96.

Rounding Things Out

Once you know a type's top two functions the others are easy to find. The tertiary process is opposite the co-pilot and the inferior process is opposite the dominant function.

Using INFJs as an example, we see that their co-pilot process is Extroverted Feeling. The opposite of this is Introverted Thinking. That makes Introverted Thinking the tertiary process.

An INFJ's dominant process is Introverted Intuition. The opposite of that is Extroverted Sensing. This means that Extroverted Sensing is an INFJ's inferior function.

To recap, here's an INFJ's function stack:
- Dominant: Introverted Intuition (abbreviated Ni)
- Co-Pilot: Extroverted Feeling (Fe)
- Tertiary: Introverted Thinking (Ti)
- Inferior: Extroverted Sensing (Se)

Becoming An INFJ

As children grow, they start to use one way of perceiving (Sensing or Intuition) and one way of judging (Thinking or Feeling) more than the other. They become comfortable with their preferred perceiving and judging functions, and learn to use them much more effectively than the neglected functions. These preferences result in four possible combinations: Sensing plus Thinking (ST), Sensing plus Feeling (SF), Intuition plus Feeling (NF), and Intuition plus Thinking (NT).

In Myers-Briggs® theory, "people create their 'type' through exercise of their individual preferences regarding perception and judgment."[13] Isabel Myers also taught that each type's function "preferences are inborn and no attempts should be made to reverse them; otherwise development may be blocked."[14]

Modern research indicates that a tendency to develop certain personality traits is inborn, but a large part of type development is also about our environment and how we choose to respond to

---

13 Myers, *Gifts Differing*, p. 9.
14 Myers, *Gifts Differing, p.* 167.

situations. For example, twin studies show that introversion-extroversion is 40-50% heritable.[15] There is a genetic component, but that's not the only thing playing a role in type development.

Whether it's inborn or developed very early in life, function preferences don't typically change. Myers-Briggs® theory does not assume that people switch personality type. If someone tests as one type and then months or years later tests as another type, it's due to a problem with the test or with how it's being taken – not a change in function preferences. We grow and develop within our personality type – not change into new personality types as we pass through different stages in life.

Not A Box

It might sound like Jungian systems like Myers-Briggs® are overly rigid in how they describe people. Sometimes when we read that personality type doesn't change we assume that type theory is about putting people in boxes. However, these type systems are meant to describe us not to define us.

Myers-Briggs® types are less about how people "should" be and more about describing us as we are. Jung himself described the psychological functions not as something he came up with but as a discovery he made about how people's personalities work.

> *"Now mind you, these four functions were not a scheme I had simply invented and applied to psychology. On the contrary, it took me quite a long time to discover them."*
>
> -Carl Jung[16]

Myers-Briggs® didn't come about as a way to force people into boxes, but as an attempt to describe how our minds naturally work. Instead of telling us who we are, it describes how we approach the world and what sort of mental tools we use. As such, the system allows for a great deal of individualization within each type. To quote Lenore Thomson, "our type does not define who we 'really

---

15 Cain, Susan. *Quiet: The Power of Introverts in A World That Can't Stop Talking.* (Crown Publishers: New York, 2012). p. 108
16 Evans, *Jung on Elementary Psychology*, p. 103

are' any more than using a particular language defines the nature of our soul."[17]

One of my favorite analogies is that our personality type is the "canvas" and our individual choices and experiences are the "paint" we each use in creating our unique lives. Even though a person's type never changes, we all go through different experiences and make different choices that influence who we become. We also go through different stages of development as we learn to use our preferred functions more effectively.[18]

Myers-Briggs® types aren't intended to put people in boxes or infringe on a person's right to self-determination. They're meant to describe some of the key categories that people tend to fall into based on how their minds work. The types are a tool for better understanding who we've already chosen to be.

---

17 Thomson, *Personality Type*, p. 23.
18 Myers, *Gifts Differing*, p. 168. Quoting Van der Hoop, 1939, p.92

Chapter Three

Worlds In My Head

An INFJ's dominant function is Introverted Intuition (Ni). As introverts, our strongest mental process is oriented to the inner world. While we do have an extroverted side, introversion is the one we're most comfortable with. Our reality is shaped from within.[19]

The way INFJs perceive reality relies heavily on our preference for Intuition over Sensing. This preference governs how we view the world, affects our perception of time, and plays a part in how likely we are to value the role of the unconscious.

Intuitive types see the world as full of possibilities, and "are comparatively uninterested in sensory reports of things as they are. Instead, Intuitives listen for the intuitions that come up from their unconscious with enticing visions of possibility."[20] We rely on what can't be directly experienced more than on what we pick up through our senses.

Dominant Introverted Intuition is characterized by its unique ability to adopt multiple perspectives. This is the function which types use to "contend with ambiguities of meaning and perception – that is, to see a situation in more than one way." For INFJ types, our primary mode of interacting with the world sees "things from many (sometimes conflicting) perspectives." [21]

---

19 "From an introverted perspective, the self cannot be defined by circumstances. On the contrary, reality is what we bring to it from within" (Thomson, *Personality Type,* p. 63).
20 Myers, *Gifts Differing*, p. 57
21 Thomson, *Personality Type,* p. 225.

Patterns, mental constructs, speculative theories, fantasies, and imagination all hold enormous significance for Introverted Intuitive types. We take these things in, process them, think about them, and fit them into our unique perceptions of how the world works. This process is almost exclusively an internal one, and it's often very difficult to explain to other people.

From a young age, most INFJs become very comfortable spending large amounts of time in their own heads, often creating their "own little world" to live in. We get used to people not understanding how our minds work and stop trying to explain a process that we ourselves don't fully understand. In many cases, INFJs end up feeling alienated from other people. We may also decide there is something wrong with us because we're so different from the other people we see around us.

This is why learning about Myers-Briggs® types is so powerful for INFJs. It's a profound relief to realize our minds are hardwired to work the way they do. Plus, the more we learn about Introverted Intuition the better we get at appreciating its strengths and learning to work with its limitations.

The Pattern-Recognition Function

My favorite description of Introverted Intuition comes from Personality Hacker. They nickname this function Perspectives because it's exceptionally good at using advanced pattern-recognition to create a meta-perspective.

Think of Introverted Intuition as something that absorbs huge amounts of information then processes it internally. In the midst of this processing, the INFJ starts to recognize patterns and then uses those patterns to come up with speculative leaps. That's how INFJs get to a point where they "just know" things. This all takes place inside our heads and results in us developing a unique perspective on how the world works.

> *"Introverted Intuition is focused on the patterns that form those perspectives, and over time it starts to see the 'pattern of the patterns'. ... This is why users of Introverted Intuition aren't married to their own perspectives. They can*

> take a meta-perspective and understand the ways in which we're the same and different on a cerebral level. The nickname 'Perspectives' seemed to at least direct people to the root of how this complex process works."[22]

Pattern-recognition and perspective-creation lie at the heart of INFJ "superpowers." Introverted Intuition gives us our greatest gifts and it's the mental process that we have the greatest potential to use and develop. Susan Storm, an INFJ and certified MBTI® practitioner, says,

> "In their healthiest form, INFJs have a deep insight into human relationships and hidden meanings. ... They see things from numerous perspectives and vantage points, which makes them open-minded and slow to judge others. To others, INFJs appear highly empathetic, idealistic, and deep."[23]

Of course, not every INFJ is in their healthiest form. Not only that, but none of us are at our best 100% of the time. INFJs (particularly more unhealthy ones) can very easily get trapped in their Intuitive side. There's always a temptation for us to stop at Introverted Intuition and never take steps toward a point where we can share our insights with the world while also appreciating the insights of others.

This tendency to get "stuck" in our favorite process is why it's so important to develop all the functions in your stack. Even if you do that, though, the dominant function is still going to be the one you use best and are the most comfortable with. Understanding how it works is vital for for growth and development, as well as for self-acceptance and confidence.

---

22 Dodge, Antonia. "Why Personality Hacker Uses Nicknames For The 8 Jungian Cognitive Functions." PersonalityHacker.com. N.p., 20 March 2015. Web. 7 July 2018.
23 Storm, Susan. "The Best And Worst Versions of Every Myers-Briggs® Personality Type." PsychologyJunkie.com. N.p., July 2018. Web. 7 July 2018.

Where We Get Our Patterns

Sometimes, people assume that Intuitive types don't pay attention to the physical, sensory world. Intuitives, especially Introverted Intuitives, are stereotyped as unrealistic, impractical, and oblivious to reality.

Like most stereotypes, this one isn't all that accurate. Even though introverts prefer to focus on their inner world instead of the outer and intuitives prefer to focus on what could be rather than what is, we're actually very observant at times. We're just not observant of everything all the time.

As we talked about in the last section, INFJs are very good at picking up on patterns. It's an unconscious process, though, particularly because our Intuition is focused inward. We might notice the most subtle body language cue that ties-in with a pattern we're constructing about how people interact, but then trip over our own feet because we weren't paying attention to something as mundane as walking.

INFJs constantly take in and process information. Much of the time, this happens without us thinking about it. When we leap to a conclusion we are often right, but in many cases we couldn't begin to explain how we arrived at the correct answer.

> *"It's also through intuition that I'm able to know what exactly to say and do to obtain the most favorable outcome for myself and for my friends who ask for advice. This prevents me from getting into unnecessary and unreasonable fights. Surprisingly, it also comes in handy during exams, because, for some reason, I have this gut feeling about knowing things that end up being right."*
>
> – Denise

Introverted Intuition tends to happen slowly and it takes the typical INFJ quite a while to feel as if they have fully processed something. At the end, or perhaps several times through this process, it's not unusual for INFJs to experience a flash of insight. Until we learn how to describe the way our mind works, we might surprise ourselves by how we "just know things" all the sudden.

We don't notice intuition happening because for us it's as natural as breathing.

Communicating Intuitive Thoughts

One of the main reasons that INFJs feel isolated from other people is because our favorite method of processing the world is hard to communicate. We don't understand how our minds work or how we "just know" things, so how could we possibly explain it to other people?

> *"I have often given up on attempting to explain my intuitions to people except when absolutely necessary or to those who understand intuition better (often times to ENTPs, they seem to get it). When I do share my true intuitions, it is often perceived as unfinished thoughts or ramblings, yet I can very clearly see the concept I am trying to convey, it is just not coming out coherently. I combat this by taking more time to process the intuition with Ti before saying it, but this often means my thoughts are left behind in a cloud of dust as the conversation flies past the original topic."*
>
> *– Chase*

One of the problems that INFJs tend to run up against is that we get frustrated by the limits of the language available to express ourselves. This is one reason I prefer writing to talking – I can edit my thoughts over and over until I find the word or phrase that expresses them correctly. When in a conversation with someone I trust to be patient and really listen, I'll do this verbally as well. It's not unusual for me to talk around an idea for a couple minutes before I arrive at my final version of what I want to say.

Unfortunately, the sorts of people who really care about understanding us seem few and far between for INFJs. More often than not, we aren't quite sure how to explain ourselves and the people we're talking to aren't patient enough to listen while we try.

> *"The INFJ has a totally unique way of seeing the world. Thanks to our difficulty in verbalizing this, they don't*

understand and give up on us. Not many have the patience to deal with us, which only fuels the feelings of isolation and loneliness that we seem to struggle with daily."

– Kerry

INFJs and INTJs both use Introverted Intuition as their primary mode of viewing the world, but INFJs are particularly vulnerable to developing a sense of alienation. We "need others' encouragement and approval to establish a positive self-image."[24] If we don't get that we start to feel isolated, alone, and different.

In many cases, we assume this alienation is our fault and the problem is that we just don't know how to connect with people. Maybe if I was better at explaining myself, we think, I'd be able to connect the same way that "normal" people do. However, the problem isn't that we're broken. It's that we process things in a fundamentally different way than most other people and communicating that is a genuine challenge.

"Introverted Intuitions are not really ideas. They're like trains at the edges of articulated knowledge. You can't claim them or advocate them. You put on a hat, grab hold of a boxcar door, and see where they go. Until these types acquire enough information to map out the path they're taking, all they can do is insist on their taking it."[25]

Until an INFJ is done processing, it's going to be really hard for us to explain what we think about something. We might feel like we have collections of half-formed thoughts more than specific ideas. And that's okay – you don't have to be sure of everything nor are you under an obligation to explain things that you don't yet understand for yourself to other people.

This is one of the challenges INFJs face when trying to stand up for ourselves. By "standing up" I mean sharing our ideas, choices, and opinions with others and not compromising on our personal standards, morals, or beliefs. For INFJs, sharing our thoughts on these sorts of topics doesn't necessarily mean picking

---

24 Thomson, *Personality Type,* p. 229.
25 Thomson, *Personality Type,* p. 229.

just one side on any given issue. We'll probably have very definite opinions on certain things that we've spent lots of time processing, but most of the time our thoughts will involve multiple (sometimes contradictory) ideas. In those cases, standing up for yourself might involve admitting you don't have just one opinion on the subject but you'd be happy to discuss several different ideas about it.

Applying Perspectives to People

Because INFJs pair their Introverted Intuition with Extroverted Feeling (which we'll talk about in the next chapter), we tend to focus on patterns that involve other people. That doesn't mean INFJ can't apply their skills to something else. In fact, many INFJs self-select into and excel at fields involving science, engineering, and mathematics.[26] However, as a general rule, we tend to care more about people-oriented patterns than impersonal ones.

Many INFJs describe themselves as empathic, sometimes to the point that they literally feel what other people feel. When we combine this with our talent for pattern-recognition and adopting different perspectives, it can look like INFJs have mind-reading abilities. In the words of an INFJ tee-shirt I saw online, "If you can read this, I'm reading your soul."

> *"Intuition is a huge part of the INFJ. We can see through fake like it's glass. If someone gives me an insincere compliment, I will know about it. If someone is trying to manipulate me, it is obvious they have ulterior motives. If someone says they're 'fine' when they really aren't, I can sense it. I can feel the anger, frustration or grief they hide behind their mask. Most of the time, I do not let on that I know these things; it kind of scares people. I can tell when someone close to me is stressed out, angry or sad without them saying a single word."*
>
> *– Kerry*

Antonia Dodge and Joel Mark Witt think the mind-reading ability of INFJs is tied to how we perceive our own thoughts. Since

---

[26] Myers, *Gifts Differing*, p. 41, 43; Thomson, *Personality Type*, p. 246.

we are so used to watching how our own minds work, we're quick to pick up on clues regarding patterns in other people's thoughts. Dodge says INFJs "get to a point where they just kinda know stuff … and because they're not really married to their own perspective they have the ability to jump inside other people's perspectives extremely well."[27]

This is one advantage to spending so much time inside our own minds. We can often guess how other people's minds work on both a conscious and unconscious level. If a person shares something that gives us insight into their thought patterns, we can use that to guess (often with a fairly high degree of accuracy) information they haven't told us directly.

Even though we call this "mind reading," it has more to do with predicting the most likely outcome based on patterns we've observed. Since INFJs are so in-tune with the behavior of other people, we can become quite good at intuiting how people will behave in the future. This has earned some INFJs a reputation for being able to predict the future.

Skills related to reading and predicting other people's behavior can show up in every aspect of our lives. For example, I stopped reading Agatha Christie's mystery books because I got so good at guessing the ending that they became boring. It wasn't because I figured out who the killer was based on clues Christie wrote into the book, though. I just became so familiar with her writing style that I was able to predict who she would choose as the killer. In the real world, being able to read people's behavior is something we INFJs rely on heavily in social situations.

> *"When I was in college, I was somehow able to pick out who the best study companion would be on the first day of class. I was usually right. More often than not, this person I picked would be a homeschooler, like me. I have kept these friends through the years."*
>
> *– Johanna*

---

[27] Episode 0034 – INFJ Personality Type Advice." *Personality Hacker Podcast.* 6 Oct. 2014

Our predictive ability is not always welcome, nor is it always a conscious process. We can tap into our intuition on-purpose to arrive at answers or to predict behavior, but in many cases our intuitive insights first show up as a "hunch," "feeling," or "gut reaction."

Even though many INFJs (including me) second-guess our intuition at times, we've learned to listen to it even when it doesn't make sense. In many cases, our intuitive side is picking up on something that is real but we just haven't consciously made sense of it yet. Most INFJs quickly learn that it's important to trust our instincts because more often than not our hunches are correct.

When You're Uncomfortable With Intuition

Though Intuition is the functions that INFJs should be most comfortable with in theory, it doesn't always work that way. Some INFJs have spent most of their lives mistrusting or trying to suppress their Intuition, typically because that's what they thought society expected.

> *"I've never really got used to intuition (I'm 64). It feels entirely subjective and only in a minority of cases do I ever know if I was right or wrong - especially if I anticipate something that doesn't happen, I can't know if my caution was the reason it didn't happen or if I was simply mistaken ...*
>
> *"I've learned the hard way to try to share [my intuitions] only after I've accumulated some observable data to support what I feel. People today are suspicious of intuition: what they want is something they can rationalise and, if necessary, justify."*
>
> *– Philip*

For INFJs who struggle with trusting their Intuitive process, learning how to incorporate it into their personality can be one of the biggest – and most rewarding – personal growth challenges. And it is a challenge. Even Carl Jung said that from an outside, rationalistic perspective Introverted Intuitives may even appear "the most useless" of personality types.[28] With that being how so much of the outside world sees us, it's little wonder that some INFJs come to believe they should repress or ignore their Intuition.

However, Jung is quick to point out that "this function, which to the outer world is the strangest of all, is as indispensable to the total psychic economy as is the corresponding human type to the psychic life of a people."[29] Introverted Intuition offers a vital perspective, and if we stamp it out (either in ourselves or as a society) we would loose something precious.

INFJs can change the world by bridging gaps between people who have different perspectives and offering a vision for what the future could look like on both personal and societal levels. But we can't do that if we try to cut-off our Intuition.

Learning to use our Intuition starts with getting to know it better, and then accepting that it is a part of you. If you can find other Intuitive personality types to spend time with, that can also help you get used to how you can use Intuition. Spending time with other Intuitives also reinforces that Intuition is both normal and useful for your personality type.

Finally, work on exercising your Intuition and learning to enjoy it. Listen to podcasts or read books that challenge you to think deeply about ideas. Start writing without editing yourself as you go. Find a hobby that touches something deep and real inside you, and then make time for it. The more you learn to appreciate and exercise your Intuition, the more comfortable you'll get with it and the better balanced your personality type will become.

Our Own Inner Worlds

As we wrap up this chapter, I want to go back to the idea that INFJs see the world very differently than most other people. Even the types that do share Introverted Intuition as a strength (INTJs and, to a lesser extent, ENFJs and ENTJs) make up a

---

28 Jung, C. G. *Psychological Types.* Trans. H.G. Baynes. Rev. ed. (Princeton: Princeton University Press, 1990). p. 404.
29 Jung, *Psychological Types,* p. 400.

comparatively small percentage of the population. It's rare that we meet people who fully share our perspective on life, the universe, and everything.[30]

INFJs rarely share our inner worlds with other people because we don't think they can understand it. That might sound stuck-up, but usually this feeling is more related to fear than pride. We've tried to explain ourselves before and we've been shut-down too often to feel comfortable trying it again. It's happened so many times that most INFJs struggle with feelings of loneliness and alienation, sometimes to the point that we wonder if we're actually human.

Still, INFJs do find ways to explore, entertain, and even share their intuitive side. For me, this mostly shows up as a life-long obsession with stories. I've always felt a bit disconnected from the "real world." Growing up with my younger sister, an INTJ, we would think up elaborate plots for our play time and act them out either with the two of us playing all the parts or (as the cast grew) with an array of beanie babies.

As we outgrew childlike-play, my stories became more elaborate and moved onto the page as novels and short stories which I now publish under a pen name. I also daydream extensively, often building stories I never intend to write down. These fantasies are often short-lived, prompted by a scene I just read in a book or saw on screen, but others are far more elaborate settings I return to again and again for years.

> *"Intuition is my savior and my escape. I can't even imagine myself without it. I always daydream and get lost in thought, especially when I've had enough of other people. Through intuition, I get to mix all my obsessions together into a perfect world in my head. It's in getting lost that I find myself free from all the stress of everyday life."*
>
> *– Denise*

Though not all INFJs call themselves writers the way I do, the practice of building stories and dreaming up worlds is something to

---

[30] Shameless *Hitchhiker's Guide To the Galaxy* reference for my fellow nerds.

which most INFJs strongly relate. It's not all fiction writing, either. There are plenty of INFJs writing non-fiction and blogs, writing in a journal where no one else can see, writing letters to friends, or arranging words in our heads without actually setting pen to paper or fingers to keyboard.

> *"Intuition has played a huge role in my life – huge! I began writing regular letters when I was 9 years old and stories when I was 12. I had a grandmother who understood me and answered every one of my letters with grace and wisdom. Through those letters I was given permission to have a healthy, active life inside my brain. I still send cards to everyone I can think of because they say they appreciate them."*
>
> – Rachel

INFJs are constantly thinking, imagining, hosting conversations in our minds, and coming up with off-the-wall solutions for problems. Often we'll stop paying attention to the world outside our heads and walk around in a Walter Mitty-like state that causes people who have no idea what's going on to label us as "crazy." It often takes a conscious effort to pull ourselves out of our own heads enough to interact with people in a normal fashion, especially if we're dealing with small-talk rather than a conversation with depth.

What makes us weird is also the source of some of our greatest gifts. One of the best things that INFJs can do for ourselves is learn to appreciate and value our intuitive side. We can't stop there, though. We also need to learn how to get out of our introverted function and reach-out to the people around us. To do that, we use our co-pilot Extroverted Feeling.

Chapter Four

Searching For Harmony

As INFJs, our co-pilot function is Extroverted Feeling (Fe). Personality Hacker nicknames this function Harmony because it's very much concerned with maintaining harmonious relationships in the outer world.

Feeling is a decision making function that we use to "organize data by relatedness to ourselves" and maintain categories of relationship in the outer world that reflect our values. Even though we typically associate Feeling functions with emotion, Jungian scholars consider Extroverted Feeling a rational process that is "conceptual and analytic." Feeling types simply analyze and conceptualize information related to human beings rather than logical and/or impersonal abstractions.[31]

Even though Extroverted Feeling is more of a mental function than an emotional one, INFJs often do experience it as emotion. We tend to be emotionally sensitive and expressive people, partly because we're so much in-tune with how people relate to each other in non-logical ways. INFJs may find that because our Feeling function is focused outward rather than in we have an easier time understanding the emotions of other people than we do our own feelings.

Feeling Others' Emotions

Pairing Extroverted Feeling with Introverted Intuition has some interesting results. Since Ni is "all about really understanding

---
31 Thomson, *Personality Type,* p. 318.

what's going on inside yours and other people's minds" and Fe is "all about understanding other people's emotional reactions and responses," putting them together in INFJs results in people who are "so sensitive to the emotions of other people that they end up absorbing other people's emotions and taking them on for themselves."[32]

> *"Speaking of emotion, I feel everything. If I see a sad story on the news, I can be sad for a good day or two. If a friend is grieving, I grieve with them. INFJs take empathy to a new level. I feel the emotions of everyone around me, even if I don't want to. I like to call it 'emotional sponge syndrome.' It can get confusing trying to sort out which of these emotions are actually mine."*
>
> *– Kerry*

Just to clarify, not all INFJs claim to be empaths. We all sense other people's emotions and feel deeply for them, but not every INFJ literally feels someone else's emotions as if they were our own. Most of the time, my own experience of Fe is more like absorbing external emotions and being affected by them, rather than literally feeling what another person is feeling.

The extent to which INFJs report feeling other people's emotions ranges from an awareness of how others are reacting to feeling like the emotions of others are so overwhelming they keep an INFJ from having emotions of their own. Some INFJs can't remember the last time they felt an emotion that didn't originate with someone else.

> *"I have a love-hate relationship with my emotions. In my circle of friends, I'm more often than not the emotional sponge. I love being an emotional sponge, as I easily empathize with people, whether they're happy or hurting. However, absorbing everyone else's emotions can be tiring, and there are times when I can't help but snap and shut down my Fe function. ... I'm very much happy for my emotions, but there are times when I question why I feel as*

---

[32] "Episode 0034." *Personality Hacker Podcast.*

such, or if such emotions are even mine."

– Denise

Some INFJs are more disconnected from feelings than others, so if you don't feel like an emotional sponge that doesn't mean you're not an INFJ. We can also purposefully try to block out other people's emotions. In addition, there are occasions when INFJs feel disconnected from their empathy even if they're not trying to block emotions. For me, this usually happens when I'm stressed, overwhelmed, and/or depressed.

Harmony In Social Situations

Because INFJs are so relationship-oriented, they're sometimes mistaken for extroverts. Introverts who use Fe (INFJs and ISFJs) are considered the most social introverts because we tend to have an easier time interacting with people. An INFJ who has worked to develop the Feeling side of their personality can often thrive in social situations, though they will still need introverted down-time to recharge.

However, just because we have Extroverted Feeling in our function stack doesn't always mean it's easy for INFJs to "come out of their shells." Many INFJs (me included) were painfully shy growing up and may struggle with social anxiety into adulthood.

Whether an INFJ is comfortable or anxious in social situations, we all share a core desire to have harmony in our relationships with other people. In addition, our deep appreciation for what other people feel makes INFJs very conscious of what is or is not acceptable socially.

Most INFJs don't like to "make waves" in social situations. We're often people-pleasers who would rather make decisions based on what will make others happy instead of on our own needs or desires. This people-pleasing side is often in conflict with our very distinctive expression of Introverted Intuition. If we decided to prioritize Extroverted Feeling and hide our Intuition, an outside observer might even mistake us for a more real-world focused type like an ISFJ.

Many INFJ struggle with a desire to express their authentic, individual self and an equally strong desire to fit-in with the conventions and expectations of people around them. More mature INFJs who learn to use their functions together typically find a way to indulge their Intuition while also balancing it with their harmony-creating Feeling to avoid conflict in their most valued relationships. It's often a delicate balance, and requires prioritizing relationships with people who let you feel safe sharing your authentic self and placing less emphasis on fitting in with everyone you meet.

Learning To Mediate Conflict

INFJs have a heightened sensitivity to conflict because of how much external emotions affect us. We place a very high value on peace and will do almost anything to preserve it. At heart, INFJs are peacemakers who want to understand opposing viewpoints so that we can create harmony.

One of the biggest growth-steps INFJs can experience is learning that sometimes conflict must be dealt with in order to have harmony. INFJs who work to develop their Extroverted Feeling can become adept at defusing conflicts and proactively working toward peace instead of just running away from tense situations.

We INFJs are very good at putting ourselves in other people's shoes, which seems to be a trait that has to do with how Fe reacts with Ni.[33] INFJs excel at seeing the different perspectives in a situation and often find themselves feeling impartial in a conflict because they can sympathize with both sides (particularly if the conflict does not involve us directly). This doesn't means we won't have strong opinions, but we often have more than one opinion about a given situation or topic.

This may be why I hate discussing politics so much. I know people who are very conservative and people who are very liberal, and no matter which one I find myself talking to I can argue the opposite viewpoint in my head. Usually I don't agree with either of

---
33 ENFJs also do this to a certain extent, but not so much ISFJs or ESFJs.

them entirely, but I nod and smile to avoid a potentially heated debate that won't change anyone's mind.

INFJs would much rather mediate conflict than stir it up. We share this trait with other FJ and NF types. All these types tend to care about cooperation and conflict resolution.

I like to think of myself as a kind of interpreter for emotion and intent because I can often help two frustrated people rephrase their arguments and come to a mutual understanding. Sometimes people get worked-up over issues that could be smoothed over with just a little help to mediate misunderstandings. The mediator role is one that I enjoy filling. It gives me a chance to use skills that come naturally to me (and other INFJs) because of how my brain works to create harmony between people.

> *"Perhaps Idealists [NF types] are given to diplomacy because they are so deeply disturbed by division and discrimination. Conflicts and controversies unsettle them, disputes and debates set them on edge."*
>
> *– David Keirsey*[34]

Of INFJs specifically, psychologist David Keirsey says they "have profound insight into the emotional needs of others, a keen intuition about buried feelings," and can help other people come to a greater understanding of themselves.[35] This skill has to do with both Intuition and Feeling. An intuitive type who uses Thinking more than Feeling (like an INTJ) might apply their Intuition to something like an engineering problem, but INFJs have little interest in problems that don't involve people. We choose to focus our energy on creating harmony and ferreting out patterns in how people work.

Processing Our Own Emotions

Since Introverted Intuition is a perceiving function and our Feeling function is extroverted, INFJs can have trouble with

---

34 Keirsey, David. *Please Understand Me II*, (Prometheus Nemesis Book Company: Del Mar 1998), p. 124.
35 Keirsey, *Please Understand Me II*, p. 127.

situations that call for introverted Judging. For example, while we can be incredibly perceptive about other people's feelings (a result of secondary Fe), figuring out our own emotions is more difficult.

The struggle to process our own emotions is made even more problematic by our empathy. Emphatic INFJs can have a hard time identifying which emotions are ours and which ones we've picked up from someone else. We know that we feel things strongly, but it takes effort to sort out exactly what we're feeling. Then it requires additional effort to learn how to experience and express our own emotions in a way that doesn't seem overwhelming or uncontrolled.

Getting our feelings outside us in some way lets us use our Extroverted Feeling to process them. This is an essential step for INFJs trying to understand their own emotions and make decisions about something. In many cases I'm not sure what it is I'm feeling, let alone how to process it, until I've extroverted my emotions in some way. Many INFJs do this by keeping a journal.

> "I get so stuck inside my own head sometimes that I want to escape but don't know how. I lose a lot of sleep when this happens. I toss and turn, and my brain is spinning at a million miles per hour with no off switch. It's like a hurricane in my head, and the debris flying around are my thoughts and feelings. It is so hard to makes sense of it all when it flies around so quickly, so out of order. It is quite a bit easier to figure out other people's emotions than it is my own, because of this hurricane swirling around in my head. Writing is the only thing that helps. I can pull the debris out of the hurricane and put it on paper. Then it can't fly around anymore, it is finally still. Only then am I able to examine it and put the pieces in an order where it makes sense. It feels just like I've taken the confusion completely out of my brain, and it can't eat me alive anymore. It is relief. It is the only way I've found to deal with such intense emotions and move on from them."
>
> – Kerry

Another option for INFJs who want to get their emotions

outside so they can deal with them is to form relationships with good listeners. One of the things I've most appreciated about seeing a counselor for my anxiety is that it gave me someone who I can safely talk with about anything and who won't get impatient with me for needing to process something externally.

I also journal about things even after talking them through with my counselor and/or a trusted friend. It just depends how much processing is required. Sometimes it takes several conversations or journaling sessions before I feel like I've adequately processed an emotion.

Without some kind of an outlet, INFJs tend to bottle-up their intense emotions. Different INFJs have different points where they "explode." Typically, we'll keep our emotions locked up inside for a long time before letting them out. But when we do finally reach the point where we feel we have to say something, our expression of emotion tends to be more violent or overwhelming than other people would expect from our typically quiet demeanor.

> *"I think that I am a rather violent and angry person, but only in my head. I feel like I want to explode quite a bit of the time, because I am not living up to my potential. But, I really don't know, I rarely let my anger out for the world to see. Maybe this is the way it is for all INFJs.*
>
> *"I tend to think about my emotions while I am having them. Sometimes, I like to imagine like I am a character from a story while I am experiencing an emotion. An example would be if I am feeling infatuated with someone who is a bit bad. I would think, 'Is this how Lucy from Dracula felt when she was allowing the vampire to suck her blood?'"*
>
> *– Johanna*

Another outlet that some INFJs use is crying for no apparent reason. We might not even know why we're crying, just that we feel so deeply it's impossible to stop the tears. The emotion that prompts our tears might even be related to something that happened weeks ago, but was only recently triggered by an apparently harmless incident.

Growth and the Co-Pilot Process

We'll talk more about how Extroverted Feeling relates to personal growth in a later chapter. For now, though, I wanted to mention that it's a common temptation for INFJs to use this function only when it's comfortable rather than stretching it to its full potential.

An INFJ might use immature Extroverted Feeling to "defensively dismiss the influence of perspectives that stop short of what they've already considered." In a sense, we use it to "protect" our favorite function of Introverted Intuition from becoming "infected" by "a custom, methodology, ideology, theory, or set of expectations that feels alien."[36]

> *"It takes deliberate effort for INJs to use their Judgment for self-criticism, and not just to analyze the limits of others' ideas. Until they learn to do this ... [e]ven INFJs, who can be seriously wounded by a rift in a relationship, are unlikely to take another's opinion of them at face value. A position that conflicts with the INJ's own is, after all, just somebody else's point of view."*
>
> – Lenore Thomson[37]

Personality Hacker calls the co-pilot function our growth position because really developing it can jump-start our personal growth and give us fuller access to the strengths of our personality type. This sort of development isn't easy, but when we start to grow Extroverted Feeling and train it in ourselves, we can start to recognize and realize our "need to be understood, to make a genuine connection with others, to be a contributing part of something outside" ourselves.[38]

One of the reasons co-pilot growth is so difficult is that most of us head for our less-developed tertiary function first. It often seems easier to go to Introverted Thinking than to do the hard work of developing our Feeling side. That's not the most healthy approach

---

36 Thomson, *Personality Type,* p. 231, 234.
37 Thomson, *Personality Type,* p. 234.
38 Thomson, *Personality Type,* p. 238.

to life, but the tertiary function does play a key role in shaping our personality type. That's what we'll talk about in the next chapter.

Chapter Five

It's Just Logical

Our tertiary function as INFJs is Introverted Thinking (Ti). Like Extroverted Feeling, this is a decision-making function. It tends to approach things from an impersonal perspective and is more concerned with accurate information than with how something will make others feel. Ti gives us a logical framework to use when sorting through what we've gathered using our Intuition.

Since our tertiary function has the same inner-world orientation as our dominant function we often feel very comfortable using it. However, it's not nearly as reliable as our dominant Introverted Intuition or even our co-pilot Extroverted Feeling.

INFJs can learn to use their Intuition and Thinking together in helpful ways that balance out our personality. For a healthy person, the tertiary function fills a recreational role. We typically start to develop it in our 20s and 30s. As we develop this function, we use it "to be playful, creative, explore, and recharge. It backs up and supports our auxiliary function and often works in tandem with it."[39]

We have to keep in mind, though, that this function can't always be trusted. "When it substitutes for our secondary function," Lenore Thomson writes, "the tertiary function will tell us exactly what we want to hear: that the conflict we're experiencing is not our fault, and that we're absolutely justified in our defensive strategies."[40]

---

[39] Storm, Susan. "How Each Myers-Briggs® Type Uses Their Tertiary Function." PsychologyJunkie.com. N.p., 20 Nov. 2017. Web. 2 Feb. 2019.

[40] Thomson, *Personality Type,* p. 98.

In this chapter, we'll talk about both healthy and unhealthy ways this function shows up. Let's start with looking at Introverted Thinking in the everyday life of a reasonably healthy INFJ.

Everyday Thinking

"Logical" usually isn't the first word most outside observers would use to describe INFJs. We INFJs, however, often experience ourselves as being more analytical than other Feeling types. Working with impersonal facts can become pretty comfortable for us even though it's not our default. We still primarily make decisions using our Feeling side to come up with harmonious solutions that benefit everyone involved, but we can also use our Thinking side to consider a more detached approach to facts.

Many INFJs who go into research or technical fields do quite well. For example, Chase (one of the contributors for this second edition) is a senior year physics major. In addition, INFJs typically score high on intelligence tests and do well academically, though Myers says this has more to do with Intuition than with our Thinking function. She adds that when INFJs are interested in technical fields, they appear to do just as well as the more analytical INTJs.[41]

> *"I'm taking up a degree in Biochemistry in college right now. In such a difficult degree, honing my Ti and keeping my Fe in the low is what I do to survive, especially in a community of undergraduates who focus more on obtaining the results than how they were obtained. There have been instances where my classmates have been, in my opinion, too cold and too analytical for my Fe function that I had to 'turn it off' in order to keep the peace in the laboratory setting. While I love the pursuits of knowledge where science and mathematics can be seen for its beauty, I can't wait to begin working as a doctor, where both functions would delight in."*
>
> *– Denise*

---

41 Myers, *Gifts Differing,* p. 66, 110.

All the TP personality types use Introverted Thinking far more comfortably than INFJs do. But even though INFJs use Ti as a tertiary function, we can still see traits of Ti showing up in INFJs. Dr. A.J. Drenth says, INFJs use Ti "to logically scrutinize and hone their Fe judgments."[42] This tends to happen more frequently and easily as INFJs mature.

An INFJ who consciously learns to access and use all their functions will develop a greater command of tertiary Ti. They'll also be able to use it more effectively than someone who ignores their Thinking side or who believes they aren't capable of logic and gives up on honing that skill.

> *"I think both thinking and feeling need to work together. I have to think of ways to make money, and then do them. My feelings tell me that I don't really like having to make money, but my thoughts tell me that I need to. My thoughts have to keep reminding me that I need to have a job, otherwise, I would be very happy just occupying myself with making crafts and then giving them away."*
>
> – Johanna

The goal of Ti is to formulate questions, create theories, find insights, and fit external facts "into the framework of the idea or theory it has created."[43] This helps explain why INFJs tend to do so well in academic fields. We love research, specifically the part about bringing facts and ideas together into a complex whole. I myself chose to complete a year-long undergraduate research project as part of my B.A. in English simply because I enjoyed doing that sort of work. It puzzled people that I would bother with that and then not apply to grad school, but I thought it made perfect sense. What was more confusing to me was that so many of my classmates would rather party and hang out with their fellow students than take on extra studies and spend time talking with our professors.

---

42 Drenth, A.J. "INFJ Personality Profile." PersonalityJunkie.com. N.p., n.d. Web. 12 June 2014.
43 Myers, *Gifts Differing*, p. 78.

Does This Make Sense?

As Isabel Myers describes it, Introverted Thinking is a subjective process that relies on impressions from the unconscious, so it works well with an INFJ's dominant function of Introverted Intuition. It is a Thinking process that is comfortable with abstract ideas, and "values facts chiefly as illustrative of proofs of the idea."[44] Ti also tends to disregard facts that don't fit with the idea we're working on, which helps contribute to the illogical INFJ stereotype even when we are using our Thinking function.

Because our Thinking function is introverted, we care more about whether or not something makes sense to us than whether or not it can be validated by an outside source. Personality Hacker nicknames this function Accuracy because its ultimate goal is to come up with "information purified from incongruities, inconsistencies and biases which produce clean concepts and an understanding of how things work."[45] For INFJs, this is a highly subjective process. Our conclusions make sense to us, but not necessarily to anyone else.

> *"It is difficult to know the difference between when I am using thinking and when I am using feeling to make decisions. It's all mixed up together in my decision making process. I make lists of pros and cons. I do research. I get advice from people I trust. I search my faith by reading the Bible and praying. I make my decision. Then I test my gut. I tell one or two trusted friends about my decision. Talking about it makes it real. If I feel sick or tired or stressed as I talk about it, I know I have made the wrong decision."*
>
> *– Rachel*

Because Ti is such a subjective process, it can help to have someone we trust fact-check us when we're basing important decisions on something that we think is logical. That sort of conversation helps us engage our dominant decision making

---

44 Myers, *Gifts Differing*, p. 78.
45 Dodge, Antonia. "Why Personality Hacker Uses Nicknames For The 8 Jungian Cognitive Functions."

process, Extroverted Feeling. Whether it's talking with a trusted friend, journaling, or some other method, mature INFJs learn to use their Feeling and Thinking together for more effective decision making.

Relaxing With Our Thinking Side

The idea of using the logical side of our personality for fun and relaxation seemed unusual to me when I first heard it. But the more I read on the topic, the more I realized this is something I do as an INFJ. I play Sudoku on my phone when I want to entertain myself. I host small parties so people can come over and play creative strategy games like Catan and Carcassonne. I read and analyze Shakespeare plays for fun.

"My thinking side fits well with my capability of seeing patterns and how things fit together. I enjoy games and activities that challenge my statistical and analytical side. I love to work with numbers and data, performing research then 'adding up' the values to determine the best option or alternative."

– Michael

This sort of thing isn't unusual for INFJs. Many love problem-solving or strategy-based games. We often enjoy studying topics in-depth and then categorizing and analyzing what we learn. In these ways, Introverted Thinking gives us a comfortable break from the functions that we tend to rely on more frequently.

"I love to process ideas. In my library I have shelves on Tolkien, Koine Greek, theology as found at Half Price Books (which I'm sure will lead mostly to abandoned rabbit trails), Romans, the Synoptics, and favorite fiction series which includes Longmire and Harry Potter. When I can clear my desk and dig in, just working though these makes me feel tremendously invigorated, and I feel like I contemplate ways to help others get things figured out."

– Roy

Another way INFJs might enjoy getting in touch with Introverted Thinking is by spending time with types who use this function more comfortably. I've talked with several INFJs who describe TP personality types (who use Ti as their dominant or co-pilot process) as the types they're most drawn to. We INFJs often find these types calming and fun to be around, and the fact that they use Ti comfortably is one reason why.

As long as we don't start relying on Ti exclusively, it can help us escape stress and find balance between our more well-developed Intuition and Feeling. To quote Lenore Thomas, "Our tertiary function is helpful and enriching when our secondary function is well developed. It provides an outlet for the 'other side' of our personality."[46]

Unhealthy Expressions of Ti

We can get "stuck" in our thinking process if we're not developing our co-pilot Feeling side or during times of stress and illness. This can also also happen when the inside of our minds just seems more interesting than what's happening in the outside world.

It's called an Ni-Ti loop when an INFJ is stuck in their introverted processes. We just skip over that pesky Extroverted Feeling and stay in the nice, comfortable world inside our own heads. When this happens, the tertiary process convinces INFJs "that they have no need to establish an investment in the outer situation." We become so tied to our own perspectives that we start to feel no one else can express truth as clearly as we can.[47]

In regards to the Ni-Ti loop, one INFJ named Mark contacted me about contributing to this book as someone struggling with "severe mental illness." He says this transformed him "from a healthy INFJ to a slightly unhealthy one" who uses his "auxiliary function of extroverted feeling as little as possible." He was kind enough to share his perspective.

> *"There are several things that I have experienced from being stuck in the Ni-Ti loop and from using Ti in an*

---
46 Thomson, *Personality Type*, p. 237.
47 Thomson, *Personality Type*, p. 237.

unhealthy way. One of those things is catastrophizing. I will get caught in a cycle of worrying and imagining everything that could go wrong from taking a particular course of action. For instance, sometimes, I will prevent myself from running an errand because I imagine all the things that could go wrong like the car breaking down.

"Also, when I get caught in the Ni-Ti loop and don't get feedback from others by using my Fe, I will come up with unrealistic ideas or plans or just wild ideas that seem reasonable to me but in fact are not realistic."

– Mark

Even though all INFJs use Introverted Thinking to a certain extent, it's not healthy to stay there as our default mode. Our most reliable function for making decisions is Extroverted Feeling and if we by-pass that our ideas can get pretty off-the-wall and we're in danger of isolating ourselves from people who would be good for us. The loop might seem comfortable, but it's not healthy in the long run.

"Another thing that happens when I get stuck in the Ni-Ti loop is that I temporarily lose the ability to see how a situation or idea would look from someone else's perspective. Normally, when I used Fe in the past, I was more aware of how other people would react to an idea or situation, but when I get caught in the Ni-Ti loop, I lose the ability to focus on others and their thoughts and feelings."

– Mark

All INFJs, not just the unhealthy ones, can struggle with this to a certain extent. It often feels safer and easier to stay in the loop than to engage with the outer world using our extroverted process.

Getting Unstuck From Thinking

INFJs can learn to use the loop to their advantage. For example, I've found that if I'm in a stressful situation that demands quick action (such as deciding whether or not to take someone to a hospital), I can take in information through Introverted Intuition and loop it through Introverted Thinking to quickly come up with a logical course of action. In short-term situations like that, it's useful to bypass my usual decision-making function of Fe that wants to take the time to reach a consensus with the people around me before taking action.

However, Ti also has a "tendency to generate self-doubt."[48] INFJs are most comfortable and confident when Ni-Fe are working together. Being in an Ni-Ti loop makes us more analytical, but it's an underdeveloped form of this analytical process.

Getting unstuck from the Ni-Ti loop typically requires going to our Extroverted Feeling function. We need to force ourselves to get out of our heads and start using our co-pilot to engage with the outer world if we want to get back to a healthy balance.

When we rely on our Tertiary process too heavily, we can become hyper-sensitive to anyone criticizing our ideas. We might react defensively and start to regard other people and their ideas as adversaries. We can also become critical of ourselves and/or come up with excuses for why we shouldn't have to engage with the real world. Both make it harder for us to take action and we may become more indecisive than usual. This problem becomes even more pronounced if we fall into "the grip" of our inferior process, Extroverted Sensing.

---

48 Drenth, "INFJ Personality Profile."

Chapter Six

The Dark Side

The last function we're going to talk about is our inferior function. As INFJs, this is is Extroverted Sensing (Se). Types with dominant Se use it effectively, but because inferior functions are underdeveloped INFJs have a very hard time when forced to use Sensing.

Each type has access to this fourth function in our stack, but it's not always under our conscious control. I love that Personality Hacker calls this the 3-year-old in their Car Model. An INFJ's Extroverted Sensing is very much like a 3-year-old in the back seat of a car. When the kid is happy you can enjoy their company or ignore them for most of the drive. But when something triggers the 3-year-old, they're going to demand a huge amount of attention and stress you out.

On a small level, making a "Sensing mistake" that involves facts or details can make INFJs "annoyed or defensive."[49] On a larger level, times of stress trigger what Naomi Quenk calls a "grip experience," where the inferior function takes over. Sensing can also show up when we're not stressed, and influences us more than we usually realize.

Quenk is a licensed psychologist and Ph.D who wrote *Was That Really Me? How Everyday Stress Brings Out Our Hidden Personalities*. It's one of the best books out there on how Myers-Briggs® types respond to stress and I'll be referencing her work

---

49 Quenk, Naomi L. *Was That Really Me? How Everyday Stress Brings Out Our Hidden Personalities* (Mountain View: Davis-Black Publishing 2002), p. 192.

quite a bit in this chapter. Another excellent resource is *Tranquility By Type: Stress Relief Tips for Your Unique Personality Type* by Susan Storm. I highly recommend both if you want to learn more about how your type responds to stress.

What Stresses Us Out

INFJs tend to become stressed when they feel overwhelmed, unappreciated, and out of control. Here's a list of things that typically stress INFJs out.[50]

- Too much sensory stimulation.
- Being overwhelmed by too many tasks or details.
- Outside interruptions.
- Spending too much time in the outer world.
- Criticism and/or lack of appreciation.
- Unfamiliar environments and/or groups of people.
- Things not going according to plan.
- Lack of harmony in relationships.
- Pressure to conform to someone else ideas, schedules, etc.

I also asked my contributors for the second edition of this book to describe what stresses them out so much that they start acting unlike their normal selves. Their list provides specific, personal examples of how INFJs experience common stressors.

- "More tasks that I can seemingly handle" (Jordan) and "Working to someone else's timeline" (Michael).
- "A negative comment directed towards me" (Jordan).
- "Not being able to get predictable recharge and processing time" (Roy).
- Operating "at a high level of social interaction for a long period of time without a mental break" (Roy) and being in "loud environments with lots of people" (Chase).
- "Loud, assertive people who can't or won't explain their points of view" (Philip) and "people who make insensitive

---

[50] Part of this list is adapted from a similar list in Susan Storm's book *Tranquility By Type: Stress Relief Tips for Your Unique Personality Type*. (2016). Kindle Edition. Chapter 3.

comments or aggressively present thoughts/ideas that are extremely close minded and refuse to acknowledge any possibility of being wrong" (Chase).
- "People who question my intentions by assuming they know why I am doing something without confirming it." (Chase)
- "Being forced to make a decision quickly" (Michael)
- "Being tired" (Philip) and "A lack of sleep" (Michael)

For many INFJs, the everyday world is a minefield of stressful experiences. We INFJs can be pretty resilient, but we also get stressed-out easily. We just might not immediately show how much that stress is affecting us.

Making things worse, neither of our two most comfortable functions is very good at dealing with inner or outer turmoil. Introverted Intuition is not hard-wired to solve problems of this sort and Extroverted Feeling is better able to work with other people's emotions than our own.

Managing stress tends to take quite a bit of time and energy for INFJs. And when we don't have the tools to manage it effectively, things just keep getting worse.

Not Quite Ourselves

For INFJs (and INTJs, who share Se as an inferior function), stress causes an "obsessive focus on external data," an "overindulgence in sensual pleasure," and an "adversarial attitude toward the outer world." The first one can make us irritable and obsessive. The second often takes the form of overeating, shopping for things we don't need, and generally becoming self-centered. The third is a defensive response to feeling like the entire world is spinning out of control.[51]

> *"Oftentimes, food is my coping mechanism for stress. It has to be good food, or else I'd rather not eat. Speaking of not eating, there have been times when I was so stressed that I lost my appetite and go on for days only eating one meal a*

---

51 Quenk, *Was That Really Me?*, p. 198.

day, in contrast to overeating when stressed. My Se function isn't too catastrophic when I'm stressed, however, since wanting to explore the world with my five senses has always been a part of me. It just all goes down to how much or how little I want."

– Denise

For me personally, when I'm "in the grip" of Se I obsessively make lists and charts, clean the house, back-up my computer, re-organize my closets, and sort all my CDs by genre, artist, and release date (yes, this actually happened). I eat sugary food, and breads, muffins, or pastries if there are any around. I'll also go shopping online and buy things I later discover I don't need (though my feelings of guilt prevent me from spending problematic amounts of money). I want to shut myself off from the world, and if I can't do that I start snapping at people for no apparent reason.

"When stressed, I find myself cleaning the house. Well, more like attacking it. I take out my anger on the dirty dishes and floors. If my emotions are a complete mess, at least my damn house can be clean! I also turn to alcohol. I will chug whiskey like it's water. Of course, I have to be pretty upset for this to happen. Usually it is triggered by conflict, and that is not something I know how to deal with. It pushes me over the edge. I clean to channel my angry energy into something productive...to feel like something in my life is in order. I drink to numb the extreme intensity of my emotions. Strangely, the alcohol somehow helps me verbalize my emotions. It takes away that wall that I put up, so I am very honest, and it gets my talkative juices flowing so I can speak freer and easier. ... I rarely get drunk, however. I don't like to be that out of control and self-indulgent. I know my limits, and I abide by those. On the rare occasion that I do get drunk, it is definitely my Se spinning out of control."

– Kerry

What we've seen in Denise, mine, and Kerry's descriptions is not how most INFJs behave "normally." They're the sort of experiences that have us asking, "Was that really me?" and "Why did I do those things?" It can be confusing – and even shame-inducing – if you don't know what's going on.

Unusual Anger

Another thing Quenk mentions in her book is that anger often accompanies an eruption of inferior Se. Though normally peaceful and harmonious, INFJs can develop quite a temper when they're pushed too far. She writes,

> *"The altered state of any inferior function is typically accompanied by a lessening of social controls and therefore more frequent expressions of anger. However, the character of that anger may be different for different types. For INTJs and INFJs, the 'cause' of distress is often one or more 'objects' in the environment. The anger directed at either things or people may therefore be more focused, intense, and extreme than with other inferior functions."*[52]

This focused, intense anger often causes us to lash out at whoever or whatever is conveniently nearby whether or not they were the cause of the initial distress. It is a tendency I'm not proud of. Perhaps more than any other way that Se shows up when we're under stress, this is one that INFJs need to guard against. It can cause horrible damage relationships that we would normally walk over hot coals to keep intact.

Looking back on when I started college, I think I was having a "grip experience" for the entire 10 weeks of my first quarter. Academically I was fine, but homeschooling had not prepared me for classroom settings, constantly being around others students, dealing with multiple professors, and adjusting to a new environment. It was just too many INFJ stressors all happening at once. I'd hold it together all day and either start crying or snap at my sister as soon as I walked through the door at home. It affected

---

52 Quenk, *Was That Really Me?*, p. 201.

our relationship for quite some time because she was hurt and confused by how angry I seemed. It's a wonder my mother was able to convince me to go back for a second quarter, but I'm glad she did. This time I knew what to expect and I loved the classes I was taking (which quickly led to me declaring an English major). It just took me some time to return to normal.

Returning to Normal

When I'm stressed out in the way we've been describing above, what I most want to do is hide in a dark room in a tent of blankets listening to soothing music and quite possibly crying. I want to be left alone, but I also want to know that people who I feel comfortable around are there to listen and help if I want.

The key word here is "if." Interference at the wrong time is unwelcome and feels threatening. Unfortunately, I expect people to be able to sense when I want them to talk to me, rather than actually telling them I need to talk. Apparently this is "normal" for INFJs, at least in the sense that it's how INFJs typically respond. Naomi Quenk writes,

> *"a period of solitude and silent, nonintrusive acceptance from others is important in their return to equilibrium. INFJs may welcome more direct support, empathy, affirmation, and acceptance, but they are unlikely to let others know what they need when they need it."*[53]

In addition to getting some alone time and talking when you're ready, physical activity can be a big help. For me, this often takes the form of yoga, which also helps me calm down and forces me to focus on something other than what triggered my stress. The key is to engage in some kind of activity that breaks the cycle of negativity. Go for a walk, get a good night's sleep, or try watching a movie.

INFJs usually need to be in places with low amounts of sensory stimulation when they're working through stress. If the lights are too bright, the noises too loud, or the area is too crowded it's hard

---

53 Quenk, *Was That Really Me?*, p. 207

for us to de-stress. Getting out in nature, writing in a journal, and saying "no" to non-essential activities will help. Also, according to the MBTI® manual, INFJs are one of the types most likely to find "speaking to a professional" counselor extremely helpful.[54]

It's also important that you try not to be too hard on yourself as you return to normal and look back on your actions while in the grip. There may be things you have to apologize for, but try to view it as a learning experience rather than "as a sign of unacceptable personal imperfections."[55] You are, after all, only human.

Righteous Indignation

A different kind of stress reaction occurs if someone crosses one of an INFJ's deeply held beliefs. INFJs are typically slow to anger, but when they believe their anger is justified their peaceful nature quickly evaporates. This often happens when INFJs witness injustice and feel the need to say something in defense of another person.

> *"At the paper where I served as editor for three years we had a receptionist who was the nicest quietest, most respectful person you could ever meet. One day a gentleman came in and asked if we could republish an article. He handed her the article and she called me to the front. I greeted him, inspected the piece of paper and informed him that it was not possible and listed the various reasons why. He swore angrily. My protective side kicked in. 'Do not swear in front of the staff,' I said in a low voice. 'I didn't swear,' he said, sounding like a 12-year-old. I said nothing but continued to look at him as I crossed my arms. After a minute or two of silence he left the office and never came back.*
>
> *"Any place I have worked I have felt very protective of the staff. Most of the time I could do nothing to fix situations.*

---

54 Storm, *Tranquility By Type,* Chapter 3.
55 Quenk, *Was That Really Me?,* p. 207

> *But when I was editor, I did have a little power to make changes. This created a feeling of satisfaction in my day-to-day responsibilities."*
>
> *– Rachel*

INFJs hate conflict, but we are not as timid and retiring as this trait often makes us appear. We're quite ready to fight for what we care about, whether its a close friend, a group of people we sympathize with, or an idea. We have very strong opinions about what "should be," and if we see something that "should not be" we have a hard time keeping silent about it.

> *"As for standing up for what I believe in, I have been removed from several jobs because I would not go along with what they wanted. My first job was in my college's student activities. They wanted me to promote programs that went against my Christian beliefs. I was a very passive person, even more so when I started college, but I would not promote the program. So, I was then moved to a building maintenance job where I didn't have to disobey my conscience."*
>
> *– Johanna*

Most INFJs won't share their real self and inner thoughts with a casual acquaintance. We'll also go along with most conversations and suggestions (or give the appearance that we don't care) just to avoid conflict. This pattern can continue until the other person says or does something that crosses a line the INFJ has drawn in their minds. It might happen in a work situation, as Johanna describes, or in a relationship. For example, an INFJ woman might be friendly to a guy she doesn't really like up until the point where he actually asks her out.

I imagine it's pretty puzzling for people who think they're getting along with us just fine when an INFJ suddenly blurts out "I don't agree. And by the way, here's everything else you've done over the course of our relationship that irritates me." It's not the best way to deal with conflict in relationships, but it seems to be the method INFJs favor.

Befriending Our Inferior Function

Since we don't use our inferior Se effectively and it's often uncomfortable, there's a very real temptation to ignore it, bury it deep and dismiss times when it shows up as being "out of character." However, there is a role for the inferior function to play in a healthy personality.

People who use Extroverted Sensing effectively (the SP types) have "real-time kinetic" skills and respond quickly to things happening in the outer world. I'm so oblivious to the outer world that I run into doors on an almost daily basis. Even keeping track of my own hands and feet can be hard — once I wondered why my ankle hurt, and looked down to discover blood dripping from a cut I couldn't remember happening.

Things like that can be really frustrating. But if we're trying to befriend and cultivate our less-developed mental process, it's better to start out by accepting how it is than by hating the way our minds naturally work. In fact, many of us could already be using our inferior function and not realizing it. For example, an INFJ who finds baking or gardening relaxing is doing an activity that engages their senses in the outer world.

One of the best ways to start befriending your inferior function is through hobbies. I've already mentioned gardening, cooking, and yoga, which are my three favorite Sensing hobbies. Photography, sculpting, fishing, watching or participating in sports, or taking care of a pet are also good ways to engage your sensing side. Basically, anything that gets you using your five senses in a real-world, in-the-moment way will help strengthen your Sensing side.

Naomi Quenk notes that ideally, INFJs will integrate their inferior function in a positive way around midlife. INFJs who do this "are likely to find new pleasures in the environment and with people."[56] As INFJs continue to grow and mature, they have the potential to learn to live with their inferior function rather than being ruled by it when it erupts during stressful situations. The more we exercise all four functions all in a healthy way, the more balanced and stable we'll be.

---
56 Quenk, *Was That Really Me?*, p. 209

Chapter Seven

INFJ Strengths

You probably learned something about yourself or the INFJs in your life while reading through the last few chapters. Now the question is, What do you do with what you learned?

For INFJs, learning about personality types is intellectually intriguing. It's also hugely validating to learn about your type and discover there are other people like you. But that's not the only thing studying our personality type can do.

One of the most beneficial aspects of studying personality types is an increased understanding of yourself and how you relate to other people. Since self-understanding is a first step toward personal growth, researching your personality type gives you a good starting-out point for improving your life and relationships.

As we study our personality types, we can gain a better understanding of our strengths and weaknesses and also explore type-specific opportunities for personal growth. That's what we'll be talking about in this and in the next two chapters.

Why Talk About Our Strengths?

Learning about our strengths helps us realize what gifts we can access most readily. It also helps us learn to use those gifts effectively in work, interpersonal relationships, and our private lives.

We often use the strengths of our personality types so easily that we don't think of them as gifts. It's so natural for INFJs to pick up on other people's emotions, for example, that it can seem like a slightly annoying thing we do automatically rather than a unique gift we can use to relate to other people. But the strengths that are so much a part of the INFJ personality type are not common in the world at large. If we ignore our gifts or assume they are not useful, we deprive ourselves of confidence and deprive the world of our unique skills.

Some of the information in this and the next two chapters has already been covered in other parts of the book, but I felt it was important to gather it in one place. Personal growth is a passion of many INFJs, who long to understand themselves and other people. Learning more about our gifts (and in the next chapter our potential weaknesses) gives us a good ground-work for doing just that. We'll also cover some more specific personal-growth tips for INFJs in Chapter Nine.

> *"The biggest strengths of being an INFJ are: empathy, patience, problem solving capabilities, a wide spectrum of interests, the desire to try and test, a global view and perspective rather than a self-centered one, creativity, friendliness, helpfulness, generosity, altruism."*
> – Michael

Non-Verbal Skills

INFJs excel at a very particular type of communication. We are non-verbal adepts, who listen not only to what people are saying with their words but also what they are telling us with their body language. In fact, we might ignore the spoken words all together and read the subtext instead, especially when talking with people we know. It's not all that uncommon for INFJs to surprise someone they're in a conversation with by changing the subject to what the other person was thinking about instead of what they were saying.

Our talent for non-verbal communication helps INFJs step around dishonesty and shallow discussion to get to the heart of a matter. We can develop incredible listening skills that make people feel comfortable opening up to us as we absorb information about what they're saying, avoiding, and feeling.

Reaching An Audience

Just because we excel at non-verbal communication doesn't mean INFJs don't communicate in words. Since we enjoy solving human problems and focusing on future possibilities, INFJs often try to find some way of communicating with an audience.

The thought of speaking to an audience is intimidating for many INFJs, including me. But reaching an audience doesn't necessarily mean public speaking (though INFJs can become quite good at that under the right circumstances). INFJs often find ways other than in-person communication to reach their audiences, such as through writing a blog or by creating a podcast.

With our keen insight into what motivates other people, INFJs can develop a very persuasive communication style. Many INFJs focus on writing as their primary means of communication, but we also offer counsel in one-on-one or small group situations. Some INFJs turn counseling into their profession, and are often quite good at it.

INFJs also have the potential to become accomplished speakers. Most find that if they're given the opportunity to focus on something they're passionate about, then the desire to share and help others outweighs nervousness about communicating to a group. Developing our Extroverted Feeling side can also help us become more comfortable with speaking in front of people.

Passion For Improvement

INFJs need something to focus their energy on and can become passionate about a whole range of things including relationships, causes, and academic ideas. If we think it matters, we'll do everything we can to move it forward. This often happens behind the scenes because we're not all that concerned about recognition for our efforts.

> *"As an INFJ, I am always conflicted. I know what needs to be done, but am usually in no position to do or change the situation. When I am in a position to make a change for the good I do so, but no one else seems to care. This causes me*

frustration. Even though others think or even say out loud that I am wasting my time, I feel deeply that I am not. If I feel I must do something I will carry it out to the best of my ability, when no one is watching, and when no one else cares.

"Like that poor plant at work – I walked by that plant every day and it was suffering. It did not have enough sun, enough space for its roots, it was never rotated to encourage even growth, and it was too close to the front door and was never given fertilizer. So I asked my boss for permission to take it home for a week. She looked at me as though I was crazy and verbalized the thought that there was nothing wrong with the plant. But she gave me permission anyway.

"I repotted it, fertilized it, trimmed it and brought it back. After a month it had sprouted new growth and I took it upon myself to water it if it was drying and rotate it to keep the growth even. One day someone noted how nice the plant looked. 'Good thing we moved it,' they said. I tried not to laugh. The plant was in the same space it had been for years. I figured it would be pointless to say anything."

– Rachel

As perfectionists and idealists, INFJs are constantly striving to make things better. Whether it's a relationship we're invested in, a person we care about, a project we're working on, or even a houseplant INFJs won't give up until they've exhausted every possibility for improvement.

Creative Wisdom

People-oriented problem solving comes naturally to INFJs. Our intuitive side makes us insightful idea-generators, and our Feeling side encourages us to focus on issues that impact other people. When confronted with a problem, INFJs ask questions like, "How can I help others?" "In what ways we can change the world for good?" and "What we can do to promote peace between people?"

> *"[INFJs are] highly empathetic but also very logical and level headed for the most part."*
>
> – Chase

This combination of creative problem solving and an instinctive sense of what people need has led to INFJs having a reputation for being "wise." This doesn't mean INFJs are better or smarter than other types. It's just a recognition of a particular skill set that comes with a healthy version of the INFJ personality type.

Wisdom, as it applies to INFJs, refers to an intuitive insight into situations. If you ask an INFJ for advice, they are rarely at loss for an idea and, if they have enough information to work with, their advice is usually helpful. We're good at coming up with ideas other people haven't thought of and solving problems that seem to have no solution, especially if those problems have something to do with relationships. It's why one of the most common nicknames for INFJs is "The Counselor."[57]

> *"I also have a keen sense for the moods, feelings, and behaviors of others. I readily spot differences in others that are associated with their physical and mental health. I 'know' when someone isn't feeling well or being bothered by a persistent thought. I often know what someone is going to do or say before they act or speak. I don't mean this as ESP because I am often wrong.*
>
> *"Yet, very often, though the person may initially deny feeling or thinking as I suggest they are, they eventually inform me that I was right. It is not unusual for friends, family, and coworkers to come to me to ask for guidance, recommendations, and suggestions – they see me as a 'therapist' or 'counselor.'"*
>
> – Michael

---

57 This nickname was popularized by David Keirsey.

Problem Solving

INFJ problem solving abilities aren't limited to issues involving people. We can also put our favorite functions to work solving any sort of problem.

> *"We can process ideas very thoroughly and very fluidly. We can make connections to come up with solutions that are clever and innovative."*
>
> – Roy

Roy isn't the only INFJ that I talked with who described problem solving as one of the biggest strengths of this type. Michael listed "problem solving capabilities," "the desire to try and test," and "creativity" among the strengths he sees in himself and other INFJs.

We tend to think of scientific curiosity and problem-solving as something associated with logical, Thinking personality types. In reality, though, everyone can problem-solve. We just use different parts of our personality to do it. INFJs use their pattern-loving Intuition, then we support it with Feeling for interpersonal problems or Thinking for impersonal problems.

Altruism

An INFJ with well-developed Extroverted Feeling is very concerned with the people around them. INFJs are quite willing to ignore their own needs and invest their time and effort into helping the people or causes that they care about. INFJs want to know that they are having a meaningful, positive impact on other people, whether it is their immediate family members and friends or a poverty-stricken family overseas.

When they have a cause, idea, or person that they want to advance, INFJs become an unstoppable force. A service-oriented INFJ will go above-and beyond what is expected. This is a strength, but one that can easily turn into a weakness if taken to extremes. If an INFJ becomes too obsessed and outward focused, then they're at risk of overextending themselves and burning-out.

"I find myself taking responsibility for everyone's emotions, even though they are not my burden to carry. I somehow feel that it is up to me to make them happy, because no one else will. If my loved ones are not happy, neither am I. I really hate this quality; I feel it isn't healthy for my happiness to depend solely on other people. This people-pleasing aspect can get out of control if not kept in check. It is such an exhausting way to live, trying to make everyone happy and feel their emotions on top of my own."

– Kerry

Conflict Resolution

Dealing with conflicts is very hard for INFJs. However, if we do the growth-work needed to truly develop our Extroverted Feelings side we can become highly skilled at resolving conflict.

INFJs have the potential to become harmony-creators. This isn't possible, though, if we avoid conflict. True harmony comes from working through and resolving potential conflicts rather than avoiding them. In order to master conflict resolution, we have to get past the point where we're paralyzed by fear of experiencing disharmony before the conflict is resolved.

Conflict resolution isn't usually a skill that comes quickly or easily to INFJs. But our instinctive understanding of and compassion for other people really does give us a good foundation for becoming skilled at resolving conflict between different groups. We'll talk more about developing conflict-resolution skills when we get to the chapter on personal growth.

Seeing Different Perspectives

We already talked about the fact that people who use Introverted Intuition aren't always tied to just one perspective. Our mental wiring lets us adopt a meta-perspective and see things from multiple points of view. While it is possible for INFJs to become rigid in their beliefs and judgmental of those with different ideas, that's not how healthy INFJs operate.

"We give any subject that matters to us significant attention, and do an extensive degree of due diligence before we settle on conclusions. We often persuade ourselves to change our opinions and perspectives where we recognize deficiencies to our own thinking."

— Roy

Of course, this doesn't mean that INFJs never have an opinion of their own. Many do believe in objective truth, at least in certain situations. When sharing those truths, however, a typical INFJ will still be sensitive to conflicting perspectives.

"When asked for an opinion, [INFJs are] not afraid to give the truth, even if hard, but won't be crass about the delivery."

— Chase

You might have noticed that many of these INFJ strengths complement each other well. Seeing different perspectives helps with conflict resolution and creative problem solving. Our ability to reach an audience helps open doors that let our passion for improvement have a positive impact on the world. Since our strengths are all tied-in with our preferred functions, this shouldn't come as much of a surprise. Every personality type has its own strengths, and it's own ways of interacting with and improving the world.

These strengths can also have a flip-side. Often where there's potential for someone to develop a strength, there's also potential for a related and/or opposite weakness. That's what we'll talk about in this next chapter.

Chapter Eight

INFJ Weaknesses

Whenever people have something they excel at there is usually a dark side as well. Just like INFJ strengths, INFJ weaknesses are tied-in with the makeup of our personalities. Knowing about areas where we tend to struggle gives us a head-start in trying to overcome our weaknesses and puts us on-guard against letting the less-effective sides of our personality take over.

Some INFJs are really good at spotting their own weaknesses. Actually, they're sometimes too good at it, to the point that they don't even recognize their strengths. Others turn a blind-eye to their weaknesses because they're frightened by not knowing how to handle their darker side. We need to avoid both extremes.

We are not defined by our weaknesses, but pretending they don't exist won't make them go away. It will just leave us ill-equipped to deal with them. But if we learn about our weaknesses and how to overcome them, then we can more easily focus on our strengths.

A Quick Note On Type Weaknesses

Myers-Briggs® theory is designed to describe psychologically healthy individuals. The type descriptions also aren't value-laden. Introverted and Extroverted orientations are equally good, just different. The same is true of our preferences for Intuition or Sensing, Feeling or Thinking, and Judging or Perceiving. There's nothing inherently better or worse about any type.

When we're talking about INFJ weaknesses (and strengths, for that matter), it's important to remember that INFJs aren't worse (or better) than any other personality type. Also, not every INFJ is going to struggle with all these weaknesses. This chapter just describes certain less-desirable tenancies that people with the INFJ type might notice in their own lives.

I've included this chapter not to make INFJs feel bad about themselves, but to address some things we can all struggle with. I hope you find it a useful tool.

> *"The greatest weaknesses are being overly sensitive, taking too long to decide, analysis paralysis, perfectionism, becoming bored with an activity, pursuit or people, extreme need for privacy and my own space, avoidance of conflict, being emotionally unavailable, being chameleon-like, poor disciplinary skills, placing too much trust in others."*
>
> – Michael

Perfectionism and Judgment

The aspects of our personalities that let us understand people deeply also have a dark flip-side. They let INFJs know how to hurt other people. If you understand someone well enough to advise, encourage, and build them up you also understand them well enough to criticism, belittle, and tear them down.

Because our judging function is externally focused, INFJs who lose touch with their empathy and concern for others people's feelings may start focusing on the faults of others while ignoring their own. We might dismiss others' ideas, become cutting and sarcastic, or leave situations and relationships that don't measure up to our standards of perfection.

> *"[One weakness is] perfectionism according to our own standards. We have a strong drive for things to be the best that they can be, but we often don't appreciate how different our idea of what's best is against what actually is best. I doorslammed a few people when I was a young adult because they didn't meet my idea of what they should*

be aspiring to. It took a lot of years before I grew up enough to understand that people do grow and I had a lot to learn myself about how the world actually was."

– Roy

We can also turn our perfectionism against ourselves. In fact, it might be more common for INFJs to hold themselves to an impossibly high standard than for them to hold other people to a similar standard.

When INFjs do this, it might not look like "perfectionism" to other people since the standard we're holding ourselves to is a very personal one. Even so, this tendency can be very damaging for INFJs who beat themselves up for not reaching their own definition of perfection.

Indecision

INFJs see every issue from multiple points of view, and notice pros and cons to every decision. Often, there are so many details and nuances in a given situation that we have no idea what choice to make. This can happen for minor day-to-day things as well as major life-changing decisions.

Which job should I take? Do I want to read *Pride and Prejudice* or *Jane Eyre*? Which major will I choose in college? Can I throw this in the trash or should I keep it? Which politician do I vote for? Should I order chicken or beef?

Every one of these questions can seem like it has life-or-death significance, especially if we have limited time to make a decision. The more pressure people put on us to give immediate feedback, the more difficult it is for an INFJ to make decisions. If it gets bad enough, a stressed-out INFJ might simply shut down and refuse to make any decisions at all.

This can also happen in conflict situations. One of my contributors, Roy, points out that that "In conflict, we hear lots of things that we disagree with, but can't process fast enough how we would respond." Conflicts tend to flood an INFJ with lots of information delivered in an emotionally charged way that makes it very difficult for us to come up with an appropriate response. That can quickly become very frustrating for everyone involved.

> *"Weaknesses: Very harsh on myself and can fall into a trap of thinking I am worthless. Highly perfectionistic of my own morals"*
>
> – Chase

Even without external pressures, INFJs can pressure themselves into being indecisive. It's often connected to our perfectionism. We might fear making the wrong decision or worry that there's no point in taking action because we'll never get it right anyway.

Volatile Temper

INFJs have a hard time dealing with conflict and criticism, and are extremely sensitive to anything that looks like a threat to ourselves or to other people. Such an encounter can leave us devastated or provoke a surprisingly aggressive response. In fact, for all their reputation as a peaceful personality, many INFJs have a terrifying temper.

> *"I can get really angry. I stare down the person who has caused the anger. I point at them and I speak slowly in a low voice about how wrong they are or how much they have hurt someone (rarely me). As a side note: I used to fly off the handle and throw aluminum cans at walls. It made a nice satisfying noise and saved me the trouble of coming up with clever things to say in anger. If I'm really angry, I can barely speak."*
>
> – Rachel

When we feel vulnerable and attacked, our first response is either to lash out or to retreat. This can seriously damage our relationships with other people, and doesn't do us much good either.

I already mentioned that my first quarter of college classes was a particularly stressful time for me. I felt unsettled, scared, and constantly on alert. I bottled up everything I was feeling until I got home. Once there, I often "lost it" at the first person I saw, usually my poor sister. I wasn't angry with her at all, but the fact that I was shouting and slamming textbooks didn't do our friendship any good.

Sensory Struggles

INFJs often feel a tug toward sensory experiences because of our inferior Extroverted Sensing function. However, actually enjoying these experiences can be a challenge for INFJs, especially those like Chase who are also Highly Sensitive People (we'll talk more about HSPs in the next chapter).

> *"I become frustrated by having to explain why I can't attend a concert or other loud events with friends. ... Aspires to enjoy Se experiences, but often fails and gets overwhelmed."*
>
> – Chase

Another problem connected with feeling out-of-touch with the sensory, physical world is that INFJs can struggle with managing money. This doesn't mean we're wasteful spendthrifts who can't budget, though we might make impulse purchases. Rather, we don't really see the value of money unless we're starkly reminded that we need it when there isn't any to be had. For example, an INFJ might take a job that pays very little because it makes them happy or allows time for other things, then feel overwhelmed when unexpected expenses take them by surprise.

Communicating Feelings

It might seem strange to list communicating our feelings as a weakness for a Feeling type, especially since I listed communication as an INFJ strength. But the type of communication INFJs are naturally good at is typically non-verbal and/or focused on a different person. It is in regards to our own feelings and thoughts that we often have trouble communicating.

> *"INFJs weakness: have no sense of direction, often so clumsy, worst at expressing their emotions, too afraid to hurt someone, stubborn, have too high / low goal."*
>
> – Yeni

INFJs have a hard time articulating what we want to say and how we feel, especially in a spoken format. We're also hesitant to open up about our inner world. Vulnerability frightens us even through we know it's essential to building good relationships. This makes it difficult to build the sort of emotionally intimate relationships that INFJs crave.

Though we INFJs might know someone well enough to feel very close to them, we have trouble letting that person get equally close to us. For many INFJs, finding words to express how we really feel in a way that others will understand is a lifelong struggle.

> *"Perhaps the greatest weakness for me is when I'm uncomfortable around people, and slightly inapt ... I'm sure they see me as odd (if not a bit weird)."*
>
> – Philip

Unhealthy Boundaries

INFJs often struggle to maintain healthy boundaries. We tend to take it to extremes. Either we have very weak boundaries that we're reluctant to enforce or we have incredibly strong boundaries that don't let anyone in. Neither one is good for us.

If your boundaries are too "thick," then you'll cut yourself off from the type of connection with others that INFJs need in order to thrive. Instead of creating harmonious connections, you'll be cutting yourself off from others. You might become what I call a "disappearing INFJ" who vanishes from relationships for months or even years at a time, much to the surprise and confusion of the people who care about you. Mistrust can also block us from asking others for input, even when it would be helpful for us to get an outside perspective on something.

On the other hand, if your boundaries are too "thin," you'll exhaust yourself trying to maintain harmony without actually letting the people around you know what you need. You might also end up in relationships with people who aren't healthy for you. In extreme cases, the struggle to maintain good boundaries can contribute to an INFJ ending up in a relationship with someone who's manipulative or even abusive.[58]

Working on your boundaries is going to be one of the best things you can do for yourself as an INFJ. We'll cover this, and other personal growth opportunities, more in the next chapter.

---

[58] Not all INFJs will attract toxic people, and you certainly don't have to be an INFJ to end up in an unhealthy relationship. That said, "it's interesting to note that people who identify as an INFJ personality type are highly represented on forums like Psychopath Free, a support forum for survivors of narcissists, sociopaths, and psychopaths." (Arabi, Shahida, "Why The INFJ Personality Is A Favorite Target Of Narcissists." IntrovertDear.com. 17 July 2018. Web. 25 Feb. 2019.

Chapter Nine

Personal Growth

Learning about your personality type's strengths and weaknesses is a great step toward personal growth. In order to grow, it helps to know where you're starting and to have some idea of where you want to go.

However, the "where you want to go" part can be challenging to figure out, even when you do know what strengths come naturally to your type. It's all well and good for someone to say "be yourself" or "express your authenticity," but that's far too vague for most of us to actually act on.

What you want to focus on for personal growth is a very individual question. It's going to be informed by your past experiences and your future goals, which are unique to you and aren't always tied to your personality type.

Though I can't tell each of you reading this chapter what you should focus on for personal growth, I can offer growth goals that other INFJs have found helpful. Some of the points in this chapter will resonate with you and some won't, but I hope that having a list of suggested tips/tasks will help in your personal journey toward growing into a mature, balanced individual and example of your personality type.

Care For Yourself And Your Boundaries

As mentioned in the last chapter, INFJs often struggle to maintain healthy boundaries. When an INFJ's boundaries are unhealthy, they tend to go in one of two directions:

1. They always say "yes" to helping the people around them, rarely/never ask for what they need, and absorb everyone else's emotions.
2. They throw up such thick boundaries trying to protect themselves that they always say "no" to helping people, start to seem selfish and demanding, and they cut themselves off from connecting with others.

Half of the INFJs who I asked to share personal growth tips mentioned boundaries, either directly or with phrases like "Don't allow others to define who you are." This topic is a big deal for INFJs.

> *"Learn to set boundaries around your introversion. First off, own that you have a personality that ticks differently and offers some really unique opportunities to improve lives of those around you. Be ready to be comfortable inside your own skin even if the people around you think you think you're on Mars and the sky is red. ... you can't pretend your way out of being an INFJ, and you are going to live better if you embrace it and operate it so that it works for you whether you are able to find ways to help it make sense to those around you or not."*
>
> *– Roy*

It's vital that we INFJs learn to establish healthy boundaries, to separate our emotions from those of the people around us, and to balance self-care with other-care. These are what I consider the three most helpful growth goals for INFJs. Figuring out these three things not only helps you become healthier and better equipped to pursue personal goals, but it will also strengthen your unique gift for understanding and helping the people around you. Improving your boundaries will quite literally change your life.

I highly recommend anyone struggling to maintain healthy boundaries check out Brené Brown's books and TED talks. She's a vulnerability researcher and I've found her perspective invaluable when it comes to learning how to set and maintain appropriate boundaries.

"Daring to set boundaries is about having the courage to love ourselves, even when we risk disappointing others."

– Brené Brown[59]

INFJs often want to take care of everyone. But you have to remember that "everyone" includes you. You're allowed to take time for yourself and ask for what you need. In fact, you have to if you want to be healthy enough to truly be there for others.

We also need to be aware that it's impossible to have a healthy relationship with everyone. Many INFJs will slam the door on a friendship or relationship that's hurting them, but there are many others who will keep trying to work things out with the other person because they want (or feel obligated) to help them.

Forgiveness is a good thing. But letting people continually push through your boundaries and take advantage of you is not. In many cases, learning to establish and maintain healthy boundaries means knowing when to cut-off a relationship as well as knowing when to hold the door open for a potential reconciliation. It's a challenging balance to find, but learning to care for yourself and your boundaries is well worth the effort.

Learn To Deal With Conflict

Most INFJs like to avoid conflict whenever possible, and if we can't get away from conflict we often react with anger or tears. That's not the best way to deal with things and most INFJs recognize it's not a healthy strategy. But we're not quite sure how to go about finding better ways to deal with conflict.

Changing how we respond to conflict starts with understanding how we naturally react to conflict as INFJs. The way our brains are hard-wired makes conflict feel overwhelming for most INFJs, especially if there are raised voices or heated emotions involved. It takes a long time for INFJs to calm-down after any sort of conflict and we need to give ourselves time and space to process a confrontation. That's why it's so tempting to keep pushing conflict

---

[59] Brown, Brené. "3 Ways to Set Boundaries," Oprah.com, n.d. Web. Feb. 26, 2019.

off to an unspecified future. That strategy often back-fires on us, however.

You don't have to wait for conflicts to boil-over into a heated confrontation before trying to resolve them. This might seem obvious to some people, but for many INFJs it's empowering to realize conflicts are something you have control over. You're the one who gets to decide how you respond. In many cases, you also have the power to choose a time and place for addressing whatever issue you want to resolve.

It's usually easier to deal with conflict if you're the one who decides how and when you're going to address it. That gives you time to mentally prepare for discussing the issues that you're worried will lead to a conflict.

As an INFJ, try to avoid conflicts before big events or bedtime, since you know it will take time to process your thoughts and emotions. Find ways to channel your feelings and frustrations other than lashing out at the people around you, even if it's something like Rachel's description from a few pages ago of throwing aluminum cans at walls. If you don't speak to others in anger, then it will be easier to try and patch-things up with them later.

Also, it's important to realize that other types often don't see conflict the same way you do. Some types love a good debate, or don't feel criticism deeply. What feels like an attack to INFJs is often intended to be a healthy conversation or constructive criticism. The realization that other people aren't out to get you can help INFJs understand and deal with the need for conflict.

A Note On Conflict For Non-INFJs

If you're reading this as someone in a relationship with an INFJ, be as gentle and rational as possible when you need to confront them. Shouting puts INFJs in defensive mode and that's usually when they start reacting with anger or tears. Telling an INFJ about a problem once is usually enough – they will spend plenty of time trying to figure out a way to resolve the issue without being beaten over the head with it.

Also, if you want to maintain a relationship with the INFJ, it's important to remind them that you still care. Explain why you needed to bring this up, say you value their friendship, and maybe (if you know they'll be okay with it) give them a hug. That helps us put the conflict in perspective by framing it as a necessary step in a valued relationship instead of the end of the world.

Learn To Work With Sensors

Since Sensing is the function that INFJs have the least access to, there is a pretty good chance of misunderstandings arising between INFJs and Sensing types. This is particularly true in interactions with types that use Sensing as their primary function (ISFJ, ISTJ, ESTP, and ESFP).

Misunderstandings with Sensing types are most likely the interactions that result in INFJs being called "too sensitive," "crazy," "unstable, or "out there." But since Sensing types make up the majority of the population, INFJs eventually have to learn how to interact with them, preferably in a positive way. We can't ignore or dismiss 70% of the population just because we process the world differently and have trouble understanding each other.

This is where researching other Myers-Briggs® types is useful. You can't force other people to study typology and educate themselves about how to deal with INFJs. But you can use Myers-Briggs® types as a tool to help you understand other people. It can give you insight into how others think, what makes them come alive, what stresses them out, and other information that helps you relate to a wider variety of people.

You don't even have to know someone's specific type in order to develop a better appreciation for the ways that they're different than you. Even a general knowledge of type theory can help us respond to different points of view in a way that's more understanding and less defensive.

One example of a Sensing-Intuition conflict is how the different types view future possibilities. Intuitives thrive on theory, and tend to look at time as a whole or focus on what might happen in the future. Sensing types, on the other hand, are much more interested in the present or the past.

How might that show up in real life? If you're an INFJ who has to give a presentation at work, the list of new possibilities and ideas for change that seem exciting to you might seem risky to the Sensing types in the room. To convince them, you would need concrete, real-world examples of when ideas like yours have worked in the past. You could brush these Sensors off as overly paranoid or lacking vision. Or you could try to see things from their perspective and tailor your presentation accordingly. I can assure you, the latter approach will be more productive.

Learn To Live With Your Sensitivity

Sensitivity is an inherent part of the INFJ personality type, and many INFJs are also Highly Sensitive Persons (HSP). According to Dr. Elaine Aron, about 15-20% of the population is "very sensitive to stimulation," which she defines as "anything that wakes up the nervous system."[60]

People who are Highly Sensitive have a nervous system that naturally picks up subtleties in the environment that are overlooked by other types. Since they are picking up more, HSPs are more easily overwhelmed in a situation that wouldn't phase someone who is a non-HSP. You can find out if you are an HSP by taking the self-assessment on Dr. Aron's website, hsperson.com.

Whether or not you test as an HSP, the fact is that as INFJs we need to recognize our innate sensitivities not as something to be overcome, but as something that needs to be understood. It's a part of us that can't be ignored, especially if we're HSPs.

That doesn't mean we should use our sensitivity, introversion, or any other trait as an excuse for avoiding normal human interaction. Nor should we let it keep us from doing things that we love. Instead, we should learn to understand our sensitivities so we can live with them in a healthy way.

I've actually become more comfortable in social groups and new situations than I was before I learned I'm an introvert and an HSP. There are some situations I avoid because I know they'll be

---

[60] Aron, Elaine N. *The Highly Sensitive Person.* (New York: Harmony Books 1998), p. 6, 8.

intensely uncomfortable, but for the most part I've discovered ways of doing the things I want to without overwhelming myself. For example, I used to try and push myself to participate in church youth retreats the same way everyone else did and then feel disappointed in myself for not succeeding. Now, I make sure I build the things that I need in order to recharge into my plans when I'm going away for a weekend of socializing (e.g. alone time in the morning and afternoon). Not only do I feel better at the end of the event, but I actually socialize more since I'm less anxious and don't feel burned-out.

Develop Your Thinking Side

We gain greater conscious access to our Introverted Thinking as we learn to use our Intuition and Feeling together. Most INFJs have fairly well-developed Ni and Fe by the time they're in their early 20s, and they'll start to use Ti more effectively in their mid 20s or 30s.

You can consciously develop your Ti by working on tasks that exercise this function. Usually INFJs arrive at decisions using their Intuition and have a hard time giving someone else a step-by-step account of how they came up with their ideas. Writing down the specific, tangible steps that you took to arrive at a conclusion is an exercise that would help strengthen Ti.

Learning a game that requires strategy (like chess or certain video games) is another thing that can help. You might also study a controversial subject and try to weigh both sides in an impartial, unemotional way. Both these exercises (and others that engage your logical, analytical side) can help you learn to use Thinking more effectively.

One way to find out if your efforts to develop your Thinking side are working is to talk with someone who uses Thinking as their primary or secondary function. If you can explain yourself in a way that they consider logical, then you're probably using your Ti effectively. Just remember not to rely on it too much – your Extroverted Feeling is still going to be your most trustworthy decision-making function. Thinking is useful, but it shouldn't be in-charge.

> *"On the whole, I can't be led by Thinking. Of course, in many situations, especially at work, that's all there's time for, especially if we may later need to explain the basis for our decisions. But when Thinking leads me, when I puzzle over a personal issue and try to rationalise my way to a decision, I'm never quite at ease with my choices. I've learned that the closer I get to a decision point, my intuition begins to clarify (presumably because I'm accumulating and processing more relevant data) and the more at ease I am with my decisions. Moreover, a good decision can always be validated by Thinking if I think about it long enough."*
>
> *– Philip*

Strengthen Communication Skills

INFJs have the potential to become excellent communicators, both in speaking and writing. Though we are introverts, our Extroverted Feeling gives us an advantage in communicating with and relating to other people. This can make us excellent public speakers.

Personally, I'm far more comfortable blogging than speaking. However, given enough time to prepare what I am going to say and a good idea of what to expect when I deliver my presentation, I usually do pretty well speaking in public. Other INFJs who take more time to nurture this skill can become quite skilled at public speaking.

If speaking to large groups doesn't appeal to you, you can still work on strengthening your communication skills. These can include developing your writing skills, or practicing speaking to a camera or microphone, or spending more time interacting with small groups or single individuals.

> *"Don't allow yourself to use introversion as a crutch or an excuse, you NEED social interaction! Even if it is really hard, push yourself and seek that discomfort as you will*

grow in self confidence and social intelligence by doing so. You will also find more potential close friendships!"

– Chase

In interpersonal relationships, try to let yourself open up to people a little more. Learn to recognize safe relationships and let others get to know you. INFJs are often accused of pushing people away, even though we long for deep relationships with others. We need to let ourselves take the risk of opening up to someone and being ourselves around them so we can reap the rewards of genuine friendship.

I probably should to take this advice more often myself, but I do have a few people who I am close to and feel like I can talk with them about anything. I am so thankful for those relationships. They've proven to me that it really is worth it to let a few people into your close-friend group.

Get Comfortable With Your Sensing Side

Though Extroverted Sensing is an INFJs inferior function, it is possible to become more comfortable with Sensing. Most INFJs don't start to develop their Sensing side until mid-life, but you can start working on it any time you like.

One of the ways Naomi Quenk suggests INFJs might relax their more dominant functions and tap into their Sensing side is by enjoying "such sensual pleasures as eating, exercising, and gardening."[61] When you become absorbed in escapist reading, are enthralled by the sound of a bird singing, or take the time to thoroughly enjoy a favorite food, you are exercising your Sensing side.

Quenk adds, "Using Sensing for relaxation seems to be particularly enjoyable because there is no pressure to achieve any particular goal."[62] An activity that makes you focus on the present moment, but doesn't demand perfection, is the sort of thing you're looking for.

---

61 Quenk, *Was That Really Me?*, p. 194.
62 Quenk, *Was That Really Me?*, p. 194.

Yoga, kayaking, gardening, cooking, and painting are all examples of my Sensing-related hobbies that I enjoy relaxing into. If I'm not flexible enough for a yoga pose I want to do, I'll wait a few days and try again. If one of my plants spreads to another part of the garden, I usually let the new plant stay. If I'm painting, I end up with paint spatters up to my elbows and just keep working on the piece on-and-off until it looks right without following any sort of schedule. I highly recommend other INFJs also find a healthy outlet for their Se that fits their unique personality.

A Word On Mental Health

In general, I think the personal growth goals I've outlined in this chapter are ones that INFJs can benefit from working on. They might not all resonate with you, but I hope you found something useful.

Before we leave this topic, I want to encourage INFJs who are working through specific issues or focusing on growth in a certain area to seek out counseling. Personally, I've found working with a professional counselor helpful not only for managing my anxiety and depression but also for increasing confidence and meeting other goals related to personal growth.

Even if you're not dealing with a mental health condition, there are other valid reasons to seek out counseling. For example, getting help with achieving personal goals or wanting someone to talk with are perfectly good reasons to contact a counselor.

If you suspect that you do have a mental health issue (not every INFJ struggles in this area, but some of us do), my advice is go see a therapist, counselor, or other psychology/medical professional. I can assure you from experience that trying to deal with a mental health issue on your own is not a good idea. Please go get proper help.

Also, I want to encourage you to remember that if you do get a diagnosis that it's a starting point for treatment, not a sentence or judgment on who you are. You wouldn't feel ashamed about finding out you have lyme disease or a heart condition, and there shouldn't be a stigma against mental health problems either.

Chapter Ten

Things INFJs Want Others To Know

Looking at individual functions used by INFJs gives a pretty good picture of how INFJs think, but it doesn't show everything. We've already touched on this point in discussing how INFJs use Ni differently than INTJs do, and how we use Fe differently than ISFJs. We have to take into consideration how all a type's preferences work together, not just what the functions look like in isolation.

The interaction of Ni, Fe, Ti, and Se form a personality that is remarkable both for how varied it is and how consistent. When INFJs read descriptions of their type written by a fellow INFJ, a typical response is, "Finally, someone who thinks just like me!" However, not every INFJ is a cookie-cutter image of their INFJ neighbors. For example, though our type is often described as "spiritual" some INFJs are religious and some are atheist.

It's important to remember that there's plenty of variation within individuals of the same personality type. That said, there are also things common to most INFJs which we don't (generally) share with other personality types.

This chapter is all about things that are important aspects of the INFJ personality type which we want others to know and understand about us. INFJs are typically very willing to see things from another person's perspective, but it's more rare that we encounter people who want to understand things from our perspective. If someone did ask us what we'd like them to know about us, here's a look into what we would say.

We're Easily Hurt

When you feel everything as deeply as INFJs do, there is a great potential for hurt. We are very careful about who we let inside. Even people we don't know can engage our empathy, so imagine how much stronger those feelings will be if we've let ourselves become emotionally invested in someone.

I worry about most people I know, particularly the ones I care about. I play out conversations with them in my head, wonder how their days are going, and fearfully imagine scenarios in which I could potentially be parted from them (especially if I was supposed to hear from them and haven't).

If something actually happens to damage the friendship, it is truly painful. I might not sever ties with someone who hurts me, but I'll feel like I can't share myself with them and withdraw in other ways.

> *"To Non-INFJs: You need to understand that we are tender hearts in a brutal world. Telling us how 'dramatic' and 'over sensitive' we are isn't going to change who we are, but it will change how much we trust you with ourselves. Saying words like that to us tells us a lot more about you – that you are dismissive of our feelings and that you just don't get it. If we are opening up to you at ALL, it's a really big deal. Please know that is not easy for us to let people in. Judgment and insults are the quickest ways to be pushed out of that circle of trust-and you may never be let back in. We only want to be heard and understood, we don't need you to fix it. We long to be fully accepted for who we are. If it's absolutely necessary to criticize us, please do so gently."*
>
> *– Kerry*

One of the easiest ways to hurt an INFJ is by making no effort to understand them. If an INFJ starts to open up to you and you react badly, they won't trust you again. We are very much aware of how weird aspects of our personality seem to other people, and if our efforts to share are met with negativity or dismissal we'll stop trying to connect. As INFJs mature, we can learn to accept criticism without being hurt as much, but it's not something that comes naturally to us. Our default-mode is to take everything personally.

> *"I have always been easily hurt. It has only been in the last 15 years that I have been able to let others insult me without retaliation, finally understanding that they were not insulting me on purpose, but that I was reacting to what I thought was an insult. This came about mostly because of my husband of 30-plus years who doesn't seem to care what anyone thinks of him."*
>
> – Rachel

We're Hopeless Romantics

Fear of being hurt is balanced out by an incurable hopefulness that eventually we'll find someone who understands us. One of the things that surprised me when I first started blogging was that the top two searches which led readers to my blog were "infj relationships" and "infj love." This was the case even before I wrote an article directly addressing INFJs and romantic relationships.

In romance, most INFJs are looking for a "soulmate" (though exactly what that means will vary for each individual). When David Keirsey wrote his personality theories based on the MBTI®, he suggested that each of his four personality groups would look for and be a different kind of romantic partner. He describes the Artisans (Myers' SP types) as Playmates, the Guardians (SJ types) as Helpmates, and the Rationals (NT types) as Mindmates. Idealists (NF types), like the INFJ, are described as looking for and being Soulmates.

> *"What Idealists wish for in their spouse is a Soulmate, a spouse who knows their feelings without being told of them, and who spontaneously expresses words of endearment, words that acknowledge their mate's unique identity. Idealists want the marital relationship to be, as they put it,*

'deep and meaningful,' Other types will settle for much less than this. ... suffice it to say that Idealists are asking their spouses for something most of them do not understand and do not know how to give."[63]

It's a little depressing, right? But this statement is true to a certain extent. If you read his entire chapter on Soulmates, it sounds idyllic to this INFJ. However, many INFJs know that our ideas of the "perfect partner" are unrealistic. We just have to find a balance. We don't want to unrealistically expect a good relationship to be perfect in every way, but we also don't want to settle for a relationship that isn't healthy because we think we'll never find someone who really "gets" us. There are plenty of INFJs out there in happy relationships, so don't give up hope if you're still looking.

An INFJ's romanticism is not confined just to relationships. The Oxford English Dictionary defines a Classical notion of romanticism as "Characterized or marked by, or invested with, a sense of romance ... arising from, suggestive of, or appealing to, an idealized, fantastic, or sentimental view of life or reality."[64] INFJs are fascinated by what might be, what could be, and what should be. We're romantics in every sense of the word.

We Commit Deeply

It can take a long time to get to know an INFJ well, whether the relationship is friendly or romantic. But once we let you inside our world and start thinking of you as someone we can trust, we're committed to the relationship.

Speaking specifically of romantic relationships, INFJs are one of the personality types least likely to cheat on their partner. We're also highly unlikely to get involved in a casual romance or have a one-night-stand. That sort of relationship simply has no appeal to the typical INFJ. Often, INFJs will go for long stretches of time without even going out on a date because they don't see any suitable partners available. Most of us don't date casually – if we're

---

[63] Keirsey, *Please Understand Me II,* p. 146.
[64] "romantic." Def. 4. The Oxford English Dictionary. 2nd ed. 1989. OED Online. Oxford University Press.

going to invest ourselves in someone, we want them to be a person who we think might reciprocate our desire for deep commitment.

With our gift of empathy, INFJs readily adapt themselves to taking care of the people they love. We also work hard to keep these people happy and at peace. For example, Kerry says that her relationship with her husband is the only time her " emotional sponge syndrome" is "more of a blessing than a curse."

> *"If my husband comes home from work stressed out, I can tell before he opens his mouth. I know that now is not the time to nag him about leaving his tools scattered about the house. I lend him my listening ear, make his favorite meal for dinner and maybe a massage if he is sore from being overworked. I do everything I can to make it better, and not worse. ... INFJs go above and beyond to make sure people feel loved, taken care of and accepted."*
>
> *– Kerry*

I like to think this level of commitment makes up for how hard it is to get to know INFJs. If you take the time needed to get close to us, and prove worthy of our trust, then we can be the best of friends and romantic partners.

We Struggle With Turning Thoughts Into Words

INFJs spend a lot of time thinking and we like to share our thoughts. The problem is, we have a hard time putting those thoughts into words when we're speaking, which can make us appear inarticulate or even unintelligent. We get very nervous if we're in a setting where we can't think before we speak or take the time to verbalize some disconnected ideas before giving our final answer.

If our listener starts to look confused or impatient, we become flustered and may just stop talking with our thought half-finished. It doesn't make a good impression and we're keenly aware of that. That's one reason so many of us become writers – it gives us the time we need to put our thoughts in order before we present them to other people.

> *"Also know that we kind of suck at verbalizing our thoughts and feelings. Give us time to ramble and explain before you jump to conclusions; or better yet, let us write it down. If we hesitate to answer when you ask us a question, we are NOT thinking of an excuse or making up lies; we are simply trying to find the words to describe what we are feeling. We don't think in logic, we think in feelings and symbols – those are sometimes difficult to find words for."*
>
> *– Kerry*

More than one INFJ has described themselves as a person who thinks in images rather than words. We feel like our ideas are huge, and getting them out in conversation is like trying to sift through a beach full of different-colored sand grains and connect a few of those grains in a logical, color-coordinated order. It's so much easier to take the time to write something out, re-read it, and then finally share it once we're sure it makes sense.

If we do have to talk instead of write, we prefer it to be on subjects we've already spent time thinking about. We're also more comfortable talking when we are with people who will be patient while we work through different versions of our idea until we come up with a way of accurately expressing what we think.

> *"I wish people were more open to conversations other than those about day-to-day lives. I look for people to talk to about deeper things, to analyze and reflect with. I want to explore symbols and meanings beneath the surface, because most conversations I've had only barely scratch the surface. Basically, I wish people would actually talk and converse, and not just create white noise. We've already had enough of that in the world, anyway."*
>
> *– Denise*

We Love And Fear You

We really do need people. While some introverts can thrive in solitude for quite some time, INFJs love being around people.

They might terrify us sometimes, and we do need alone time to recharge, but life without people makes us depressed. This doesn't mean you're likely to find INFJs at parties, however. It's very difficult for us to open up and be authentic when we feel overwhelmed. Many INFJs are highly sensitive to large crowds, loud noises, bright lights and a whole host of other things associated with typical gatherings of people.

> *"Now that I'm in college, I'm so surrounded by extroverts that it sometimes hurts. I sometimes feel like there's really no one I could talk to about things I want to talk about, as these people weren't ones to look into the how, why and what ifs of life. Feeling like a sore thumb, like in grade school, I reverted back into being antisocial to reserve and recharge my energy. I realized that I was more sensitive to noise, disorder, and large crowds, which my classmates are actually made of, draining me much more. I still have a small group of friends, but sometimes it feels better to be alone, as even they aren't interested in things I obsess about."*
>
> – Denise

INFJs crave deep connections and prefer a few close friendships to several superficial friends. When we can't find those types of friendships, we tend to retreat inside ourselves. When we do find the type of close friendships we crave, we want them to last forever and we'll work hard at being a good friend. Unfortunately, it is difficult for us to make these deep friendships in the first place because we're reluctant to share our true selves with others. It's taken years for me to share bits of my inner world with my closest friends.

> *"I want people to know that we are actually very interesting people and that we can have great conversations when we are in a one on one situation. It irritates me when people say that I am shy. I am not shy; I merely do not want to talk at the moment."*
>
> – Johanna

Because of our reluctance to open up to strangers or in large groups, people often assume that INFJs (and other introverts) are shy. Shyness and introversion are often confused, but introversion is an inherited preference for whether you are most comfortable in the inner world or the outer world, while shyness is a fear of social situations. INFJs can be shy, but usually we're just waiting for the right setting to reveal exactly how interesting we are.

We Really Do Want to Know You

One of the misunderstandings people frequently have about INFJs (and other introverts for that matter) is that they assume we're stuck-up and aloof. I've even see other introverts misinterpret a reserved personality in someone else as an indication that they either 1) don't have anything interesting to say, or 2) think they're better than everyone else.

INFJs tend to be pretty good at giving other people the benefit of the doubt and trying to see things from the other persons perspective. And we really appreciate it when others do the same for us. We don't mean to come across as aloof or uninterested in you. In fact, it's probably the exact opposite.

> *"Being somewhat aloof and reserved doesn't mean we don't want to get to know you or vice versa. We just want someone who will at least try to understand us, and that is enough. Also not remembering your name is not a sign we didn't value the conversation we had, but details just aren't our thing."*
>
> – Chase

INFJs can be really observant about some things and spectacularly oblivious about others. We might remember the most detailed trivia you shared about your past without remembering your name or maybe even what your face looks like (at least not if we've only met you once).

Even if it seems like INFJs are checking-out sometimes, we really do find other people fascinating if we can get into a conversation that goes past the surface level. Unfortunately, that isn't going to happen very often if people assume we don't want them to talk with us.

We're Open Minded

Though the "J" in INFJ makes us look like a Judging type, that just refers to our extroverted function. Using Introverted Intuition as our preferred function means that INFJs are actually a dominant Perceiving type. Though we do express our judgments, an INFJ's first instinct is to sit back and observe while trying to understand what's going on from as many different points of view as we can imagine. This makes us very open minded, and we can handle just about any confidence you want to share.

> *"Don't be afraid to spill your guts to us. INFJs aren't fans of superficial conversation, we actually want to talk about something real. We crave 'real' in this world of fake, so don't feel like you have to hold back. I promise we can handle anything you have to say. Our own emotions are crazy intense, so we are used to it. Also, we won't judge you. INFJs are quite open-minded. We have the ability to see things from all perspectives; we are able to put our own opinions aside and we genuinely want to understand yours."*

– Kerry

INFJs welcome it when you're honest with them, even if it's something you think they won't like. Confession might actually make an INFJ trust you more, since we know how hard it is to open up. We love talking with someone who is interested in peeling back psychological and emotional layers, ours as well as theirs if we trust them enough. Even issues that tend to deeply polarize people are open for discussion with an INFJ.

> *"I was also more timid and soft-spoken compared to my other friends. However, I noticed that I didn't really have an opinion of my own about well... everything. My friends were pretty opinionated when it came to politics and gossip*

> *and everything else happening at the present moment, while I was never into such topics. I preferred talking about the how and the why of things, and how they'd affect the future."*
>
> *– Denise*

While we do have strong opinions on some things, most of the time we just want to talk about different ideas. When an INFJ really cares about a certain cause they may even try to convince you their view is right. However, most will still listen to your viewpoint with an open mind and try to keep the discussion peaceful. We respect diversity of opinion, even the opinions we don't like.

We're Free Spirits

Though INFJs all share certain characteristics we're also deeply individualistic, especially as we mature. We often hide our more unusual side because our Extroverted Feeling function is constantly reminding us of what is and is not socially acceptable, but it is there.

> *"I think, as an INFJ, I just want people to allow me to be myself and not try to push me into a strangely-shaped pigeon hole."*
>
> *– Rachel*

INFJs are deep and complex, but we prefer to live simple lives. Making an INFJ happy doesn't require all that much physical stuff. We delight in the little things, and love being free of the confinement that comes with having too much stuff to worry about. Possessions and money are okay, but relationships and people are far more important. We'd rather be happy than wealthy, and rather be accepted and valued for who we are than hold a prestigious job.

> *"I wish others realized that INFJs are very uncommon. That we can and frequently do take on numerous characteristics in order to fit in, but our true nature is not*

easy to discern.

"I wish there were some easy way for others to recognize us as INFJs, alas, we can't go through life where signs on our foreheads – 'Hey! Please respect me and tolerate me for what I am, an INFJ.'

"And, last, I am NEVER going to be what someone else wants me to be. I will fight and resist to my death if necessary. I am ME not you!"

– Michael

We're Always Learning

INFJs never stop learning. In academic environments, INFJs tend to be model students. We are conscientious about fulfilling class assignments, catch on quickly to what individual teachers expect, and express ourselves well in written assignments.

We are among the most likely types to pursue higher education, but even after graduating with a degree (or two, or three), we continue to study. INFJ who don't pursue higher education often continue to self-educate as well. The subjects INFJs study are as varied as they are. Popular choices tend to focus on understanding how other people think, which includes fields such as literature, psychology, and cultural studies.

Many INFJs are avid readers, consuming books on a wide range of fiction and non-fiction subjects. I usually read 50-70 books a year. My reading list includes everything from psychology studies, to Young Adult novels, to literary criticism, to sci-fi and fantasy. I particularly enjoy fiction that makes me look at the world in a new way, or consider ideas that I'd never thought about before. The INFJs I know have similarly (or even more) diverse interests.

We Want to Make The World Better

INFJs are idealists with a deep interest in people coupled with imaginative insight. So of course one of the things we most desire is to change things for the better.

"I hope they will understand a bit about INFJ's extreme changing mood & their own world and see them as something that like 'INFJs care about you, we are not trying to eat you or manipulate you, we are just trying to do the best to make a better place in world, where people can live for themselves, others and have less regrets in their own life; even though our way to show it or make it through some kind of odds, extremes, and complicate.'"

– Yeni

INFJs want acceptance from others, harmony in relationships, and the freedom to be themselves – and we want that for everyone else as well. We're a type who will counsel a complete stranger, keep checking in on a friend who confided they were struggling, or travel half-way around the world to quietly battle injustice.

Lists of famous people often typed as INFJs are full of the names of those who dedicated themselves to making the world a better place. These include Dietrich Bonhoeffer, Mohandas Gandhi, Jane Goodall, Florence Nightingale, and Eleanor Roosevelt.[65] Whether or not all these people were actually INFJs is up for debate, but they share many traits that INFJs can relate to. Whether we work quietly to change our own tiny corners of the world or step out onto a larger stage, many INFJs are strongly focused on making the world a better place.

We Need To Express Ourselves

As we touched on when discussing Extroverted Feeling, INFJs need to have an outlet for their emotions. This often takes the form of writing since we're usually more comfortable sharing our thoughts that way than in spoken words. We can also find self-expression through painting, music, photography, or some other kind of art. One INFJ, for example, runs a blog called INFJoe and shares his thoughts on the world in the form of cartoons.[66]

---

65 "INFJ Overview." Truity.com. n.d. WEB. 28 Feb. 2019.
"Idealist Counselor." Keirsey.com. n.d. WEB. 28 Feb. 2019.
66 You can find his work at https://infjoe.wordpress.com/blog/

"Intuition also helps me to visualize a project before it is created. I sew and make art. I can compose an outfit in every detail and think of every problem that could happen and how to solve it before there is anything created. When I actually begin the project, I am able to sail through it because I already have all of the problems figured out."

– Johanna

Since INFJs loath boredom, they enjoy a wide variety of hobbies that require creativity, planning, and research. Chosen hobbies often pick up on our inferior function and require some Sensing skills instead of relying solely on Intuition.

Examples of this would include gardening and cooking, which are two of my hobbies. Other hobbies that I've seen INFJs talk about include playing or composing music, listening to music, swimming, art appreciation, learning languages, playing immersive video games, and attending cultural events.

We're Not Broken

Because INFJs are so rare, our unique way of seeing the world often seems very out-of-step with what society expects. This doesn't mean there's something wrong with us. It hurts when someone assumes that we're overly sensitive, emotionally unstable, or completely impractical when we're simply processing things the way that our minds are naturally set-up to function.

While all INFJs can struggle with not fitting into society's expectations, it can be especially challenging for INFJ men. INFJs aren't the rarest type among women. In fact, quite a large percentage of women are FJ types and we can blend-in pretty well if we want to. That's not to say INFJ women won't feel out-of-place in society as a whole, but as a general rule we fit into society's expectations a bit better than our male counterparts.

Among men, INFJs are the rarest type.[67] On top of that, many Extroverted Feeling traits such as emotional availability and a

---

[67] "Estimated Frequencies of the Types in the United States Population." CAPT.org. n.d. WEB. 13 June 2019.

desire for harmony have traditionally been associated with femininity (at least in Western cultures). This can make it difficult for INFJ men to figure out how they fit in, especially in the society of other men.

> *"The stereotype of men makes me feel like I am weak if I show too much empathy to my fellow man as though we are supposed to be hard a**es all the time. This has lead to a long delay in the development of my Fe and an over development of Ti. This stereotype also makes me feel like an outsider when I despise engaging in crass conversations or other 'manly' things like weightlifting. I hate gyms, so much fakery and attention seeking narcissism."*
>
> *– Chase*

Several INFJ men I talked to said they struggled with society's expectations of how men should behave. One said he "might be seen as emotionally unstable" if he even sheds a few tears. Another talked about the difficulty of being a primary wage earner and feeling alone, as if you have to "shoulder it all in a manner that we believe we're supposed to have – but don't really have – the strength for." Another talked about relationship struggles, and the fact that "others are uncertain of my sexual orientation and leanings."

INFJs – both male and female – are not broken. We're just hardwired to process, respond, think, and feel in ways that aren't always what others expect. We want people to know that there's not something wrong with us just because we're a little different. We aren't broken. We're just INFJs.

Chapter Eleven

How Other People See INFJs

For the first edition of this book, I almost didn't write a chapter about how other people see INFJs. I have such a hard time seeing myself through other people's eyes that I didn't think I'd be able to do justice to this topic. But that's also the reason I thought this chapter would be a good addition. If I had trouble figuring out how other people see me, then maybe other INFJs also struggle with it.

INFJs are supposed to be really good at reading other people's emotions, guessing their thoughts, and seeing things from their perspectives. In many situations, that's true. But there's one type of situation where many INFJs (including myself) feel like we have a blind spot.

It's like there's a mental block when I'm trying to see myself from other people's perspectives. I have to ask my closest friends how I come across in conversations, whether or not someone's response to me was positive, and if what I said made sense. I suspect that for me personally much of this is related to social anxiety. But I've also learned that I'm also not the only INFJ who struggles with this, so I can't just explain it away as anxiety.

> *"INFJs have their own world; their own way of thinking ... the first impression INFJs show was really introvert[ed], rigid, scholar-types, aren't someone that [you] can be close with, and boring."*
>
> – Yeni

INFJs often assume that people think we're weird and that they won't like us because we're so different. That might be true of some people we meet, but it's definitely not true of all of them. I've talked with enough non-INFJs to know that quite a few actually do like us. Our INFJ weirdness isn't guaranteed to scare everyone away. In fact, what makes each of us "weird" is also what makes us attractive to the kind of people who connect well with our unique, authentic selves.

I'll be sharing some quotes from my ENFJ brother in this section (who has other INFJ friends and acquaintances besides just me), as well as referencing other non-INFJs who've commented about our type in pubic forums. With this help, I've come up with a few key points about how other types view INFJs.

I know it might seem when you're first looking over this list that people's impressions of INFJs are mostly negative. But I don't really think that's what's going on. For one thing there are several positive descriptions on this list. Plus, in many cases, the descriptions that seem negative are ways other types misinterpret how certain (but not all) INFJs interact with them. Knowing about these misinterpretations empowers us to take steps to change how other people perceive us, if that's something we'd want to do. At the very least, it gives us a glimpse into why some other people might relate to us the ways that they do.

Socially Awkward

Most INFJs either already know (or fear) that they come across as socially awkward. But while people do notice how awkward we can be, the truth is they're not judging us nearly as much as we think they are.

Others may see INFJs who aren't confident using their Extroverted Feeling side as meek, timid, or frightened. They might even assume we're aloof, uninterested, or boring. I can't tell you how many times my awkwardness has been misinterpreted as someone thinking I have no interest in them when in reality I was too nervous to engage fully.

When I was writing the first edition of *The INFJ Handbook*, my ENFJ brother – Nathan – shared with me that "INFJs seem less socially functional than they might actually be. They come across as extra shy, but seem to function pretty well once they 'get out' a little bit." In other words, we tend to worry so much about how we're coming across that we make ourselves more awkward than we need to.

> *"I would say you worry too much about talking to people. ... You usually know more about a subject you're talking about than the people you're talking to do, especially if it's something you've studied and they haven't, so you can stop being so anxious about it. And practice makes perfect. If I haven't been out of the house for a while I feel rusty and it's harder to talk to people."*
>
> *– Nathan*

It's kinda reassuring to know even extroverts can feel socially "rusty" if they don't spend enough time with other people, isn't it?

Most INFJs are better at holding conversations than they give themselves credit for, and some who learn to effectively use their Extroverted Feeling can actually be mistaken for extroverts. We really don't have as much to worry about as we think. Also, even though people notice when an INFJ feels socially awkward, most aren't looking down on us for it. They just wish we felt more relaxed.

Kind, Helpful, and Safe

INFJs don't come across as socially awkward in every situation. In fact, it's pretty common for other people to see us as friendly, kind, and easy to talk with. Depending on the situation, most of us have the ability to set people at ease and make them comfortable opening up.

There is something about being an INFJ that attracts confidences. People, especially wounded people, often pick up on the fact that INFJs are safe for them to talk with. Antonia Dodge of Personality Hacker says, "I've had INFJs say that people just instinctively know that the INFJ is going to understand them so they'll get total strangers on buses sitting down and telling them their life story. ... they're just emitting this energy of 'I get it, I get it'."[68]

From an INFJ's perspective, this can be very puzzling. We rarely (if ever) open up about our lives to new acquaintances and we have a hard time figuring out how and why we ended up comforting a stranger in the bathroom or counseling a new acquaintance who just shared their biggest struggles. To them, INFJs are a safe place to share because we tend to come across as compassionate, non-judgmental, and eager to really listen. One ENFP who I found writing about this topic said, "Some of the wisest, sweetest most helpful people I know are INFJs. ... they are like warm hugs."[69]

I vividly remember one incident at college when I sat in an unoccupied chair and started studying a textbook while eating lunch. The woman across from me, who was also studying, put down everything she was working on and interrupted my lunch to tell me all about her conflicts with her boyfriend and how their child was doing, complain about her living situation, and describe her relationship with her mother. Then she asked if I could watch her stuff and left her laptop, backpack, and purse all there with someone she'd never seen before. It seemed so strange, but it's a fairly common occurrence for INFJs.

Excessively Indirect

I saw someone online describe INFJs as "one type I'm not keen on having a relationship with" because of our conflict avoidance. Apparently, some people see us as so indirect that they don't want to go to the effort of figuring out what the "deeper meaning" is beneath what we're saying.

This puzzled me at first. After all, one of the the reasons we speak in layers of meaning is to hide things that might upset other people. However, when I asked Nathan how he felt about INFJs'

---
[68] "Episode 0034." Personality Hacker Podcast.
[69] Quote from Archana Ramanathan, MBTI certified instructor, responding to the question "What do you think about people with INFJ personalities?" Quora.com. 10 Apr 2019. WEB. 22 May 2019.

tendency to avoid speaking our minds, he said, "That is kinda annoying. You do that a lot."

The more I've talked with people about how they view INFJs, the more I've realized that our choice to hide our true feelings in order to minimize conflict is interpreted differently by others. Instead of avoiding hurt, we cause confusion. That's why I get comments on my blog from people who can't figure out whether or not an INFJ likes them or who are confused by an INFJ who seemed friendly and then vanished.

Realizing we come across as too indirect might actually be a relief for INFJs. I know I have a tendency to talk in circles sometimes because I try to soften anything that might seem harsh and to make sure I've fully explained my ideas. But really, it's okay to just say what we want to say in a more direct fashion. There's a good chance that something you think is too blunt will seem normal to other people.

Intense

People often assume when they first meet an INFJ that their new acquaintance is gentle, kind, naive, and perhaps even timid or submissive. I've been described as "gracious," "polite," and "a calming presence." People I don't know well routinely refer to me by pet-terms like "honey" or talk to me as if I'm a child. If I don't want someone to get close, I usually let this initial impression continue. For INFJs who do this, it's like wearing a mask to keep others from getting to know who we really are.

It's only when people get to know us, or witness us reacting to something we're passionate about, that they get a taste of exactly how deep INFJ emotions run. I've even had people describe me as "intimidating." When people find out about INFJ intensity, it can either scare them off or make them even more interested in getting to know us.

> *" I am very passionate and can get overly excited about what I truly enjoy. To the point that I tend to get louder the more excited I am about a topic. People usually have to tell me to calm my pipes."*

– Jordan

We probably don't want to get close to people who aren't comfortable when we share our inner self. But we should also be aware of how our intensity can come across to others.

On the one hand, certain people admire INFJs' passionate natures. They see us as generous, caring, and sincere. They admire how alive we seem when talking about something we care about or fighting for a cause we believe in. When people connect with an INFJ's intensity and passion on a personal level, they might even start to see the INFJ as a leader.

On the other hand, some people describe INFJs as "too sensitive," "too intense, "crazy," or "unstable." These sorts of descriptions typically come from types that clash with INFJs on the Sensing or Thinking preference. But even when there's less of a difference in personality preferences, INFJs can still come across as overly idealistic.

Some people will try to cure an INFJ of their idealism and intensity, or they might just walk out of the relationship. It's important for INFJs to realize what's going on when this happens. If we want to preserve a relationship with someone like this, we might need to tone-down our emotional reactions, at least until we know them better. But there are also times when we simply have to let people go if they aren't willing to accept who we are.

Arrogant

This one definitely isn't going to apply to all INFJs, but it can be an issue. Sometimes excessively indirect INFJs come across as passive-aggressive and/or as taking pride in how hard it is for others to understand them. Our intensity related to certain topics can also make us seem arrogant, though this is usually not the INFJ's intention.

INFJs often speak with multiple layers of symbolism, but we don't always know how to explain how we came to our conclusions. We hope/expect other people to just "get it." If they don't understand what we're trying to say, our reaction may leave them with the impression that we feel superior to them.

"When you're talking about something, and you think you've already figured out where the conversation is going, sometimes you act like, 'I'm done with this you need to shut up.' And if you think something is stupid you get grouchy with it. Sometimes you come across as really superior."

– Nathan

I'm certainly not saying INFJs need to stop using their intelligence or talking about their passions to avoid stepping on people's toes. But if we're consistently coming across as arrogant and we don't mean to, then we might want to take a look at why that's happening and take steps to change how we present ourselves.

Their Favorite Type

While no personality type is objectively "better" than any other type, many of us do have some types that we connect with more easily and tend to appreciate more than others. And in the context of this chapter, I think it's well worth noting that INFJs are some people's favorite type.

There really are people out there who see your INFJ weirdness as attractive or even fascinating. They recognize and appreciate INFJs' intelligence, caring nature, sense of humor, and sincere kindness.

Because INFJs are such good listeners, we're also attractive to anyone who wants or needs someone to talk to. Many people love INFJs because we make them feel valued and heard. They also appreciate the perspective and the counsel that we can offer.

In addition, while some people find INFJ intensity and depth intimidating, others find it intriguing. Other types often describe us as mysterious or enigmatic, and those traits can be very attractive to certain personalities. This is probably why most type psychologists suggest INFJs pair with other Intuitive types for romance and friendship, since Intuitives are more lively to be attracted to shared ideas and deep discussions.

INFJs are also open to bonding deeply with other people,

which is very attractive to types who like to "go deep" in relationships. That's good for us, since INFJs enjoy connecting with people on a deeper level and want to be seen and appreciated. So take heart – there are people out there who love your uniqueness!

Afterword

I hope reading this book has given you a better understanding of INFJs, whether this is your own personality type or you're seeking a better understanding of the INFJs in your life.

The last thought I want to leave you with is this: INFJs are rare, which makes their unique gifts that much more valuable. Feeling like we're so different from the other 99% of the world's population is not easy, but if we let the fear and pain of being rejected or misunderstood drive us into hiding we deprive ourselves of incredible opportunities for growth and we rob the world of our insight and empathy.

INFJs who use their gifts can literally change the world. Mahatma Ghandi and Mother Theresa were most likely INFJs, as were poet Emily Dickenson and psychologist Carl Jung.[70] Without them, India's struggle for freedom might not have been based on non-violent principles, many more poor people would have been without homes, whole collections of beautiful poetry wouldn't exist, and we would not have the psychology theories that led to Myers-Briggs® typology. Your contributions as an INFJ might not be so widely visible as theirs, but they can be just as valuable.

---

70 Keirsey, David. "Well-Known Idealists (NF)." Keirsey.com. N.p., n.d. Web. 2 Dec. 2014.

About The Author

Marissa Baker is a writer and blogger with a passion for psychology, personality types, and helping people reach their full potential. She is a homeschool graduate with a B.A. in English from The Ohio State University. You can find Marissa online at LikeAnAnchor.com, where she explores topics of personal growth and development from a Christian perspective.